SANDRA HASELEY &
SHIRAN COHEN

GRIT & GRACE

Twelve Empowering and True Stories Authored By Women Who Found Strength and Hope During Times Of Darkness and Despair

GRIT & GRACE

Storytelling editing: Sandra Haseley

Editing: Diane Kaye

Cover Design: Okky Cahyana

CHAPTER OUTLINE

SCAN THE QR CODE BELOW TO

BE THE FIRST TO KNOW ABOUT

EVERYTHING GRIT & GRACE!

DEDICATION

To Cameron Ava, my legacy and my pride. I pray you never stop seeking truth and wisdom, that you'll always grow in compassion for others, and that you'll always have powerful women to support and encourage you.

-Sandra Haseley

To YOU, wonderful lady, who is reading the inspiring stories of the twelve powerful women in this book. May you find strength and happiness every day.

-Shiran Cohen

INTRODUCTION

We don't volunteer for hardships in life, but we're also not ignorant enough to imagine they won't show up. We *know* the gritty part of life will come, but along with it, we get to choose to believe that the grace will show up, too. And as long as we look for it, we don't have to face our lives with the same fear we used to. We feel steadier and more powerful in the face of whatever challenge we confront.

One of the most effective ways in history to enhance that level of steadiness, understanding, and trust is the ability to share our stories of grit and grace with the people in our lives; to give them strength and tools to arm themselves for their next unknown struggle.

Our intention, through this collection of stories, is to help you borrow strength from the women who have been there before you as they offer their best insight to the grace that's available to us all.

When you've planned your best, made informed decisions, took care of what you could… well that's actually the very best you can do. The rest can't be up to you, so instead, you get to sit back and expect to see some form of grace appear in all of it, because you *know* it'll be there if you're brave enough to look.

When we're going through challenges that feel like they might be the darkest thing we ever face, the pain, sadness, or hopelessness can feel overwhelming. But we encourage you to look for the treasure *anyway*.

Because in order to achieve purified gold, the temperature of the fire needs to be nearly two thousand degrees.

Some of the most luxurious oils are made by forceful extraction, while destroying the olives.

Extreme pressure and lifetimes of waiting is required for the earth to naturally create the world's most valuable diamonds.

Grapes are gathered while they're ripe and later smashed in order to harvest the richest wines, leaving only the remains of what *used* to be a grape.

None of the luxury items mentioned developed their value or quality overnight, and you're no different. It takes time for your transformation to process, while the enhanced version of you is forged; creating a unique and more powerful version of your former self.

You've been through grit before, you've been through SO much grit since, and you'll go through so much more before you've completed your work on this planet. But the more grit you experience, the more resilient you become. The more wisdom you gain, the more valuable you are to others as a result.

The endurance, the faith, the ability to stay grateful, and the willingness to serve others through it are what make you a walking testimony to the people in your life that need a little hope that they can get through their next hard thing, too. Sharing the experience that was so hard for you and letting that be a guiding light, a warning lesson, or a tale of encouragement for someone else means that the sacrifice or suffering you went through can't go down in history as "bad". You flipped the script on it and reframed your challenges for good by leveraging it for something better. The story and your experience served a purpose.

And hey, feel free to use the chapter index more like a menu; take what you need when you need it, or if your appetite is big, eat the whole 12-course meal, girl!

This author's alliance that we have created within Grit & Grace is a community of women who know, love, and respect each other. It is our intention to invite women to connect with any of the authors you feel led to. Consider this book an open door to create more conversation, share stories, and expand our collective wisdom. We've each witnessed, first hand, the extraordinary impact women have made when they intentionally come together for a powerful purpose.

Due to the heart and purpose of this book, there are sponsors that have aligned with certain authors to endorse the message to ensure a greater reach for this book to get into more hands who need it. Just like they believe in Grit & Grace, we believe in them, their values, and their willingness to support the empowerment of women everywhere. So if you're also all about supporting incredible change-makers, visit the back of this book and get to know some of the hearts behind this message.

On behalf of all of the authors of Grit & Grace, we welcome you to our stories and we're so glad you're here.

CHAPTER 1: FALLING APART FOR FAITH

By: Sandra Haseley

I sat there with my knee bouncing up and down as it often did when I was anxious or full of nerves.

Hadn't it been like 15 minutes since the doctor left and said she'd be right back? How long does "conferring" with another doctor take for something like this?

After a week of random and intermittent fever spikes along with highly unattractive and agonizing welts on my skin, I went into the campus emergency clinic hoping for some answers and potential relief. Not to seem too needy or anything, but it was extremely painful, plus, skin welts and fever sweats are kinda hard to disguise from the ever-judgmental co-eds, ya know?

The doctor came back in and decided that she didn't actually know what was going on and neither did her colleague.

Cool, so I'll just, what…drink more fluids and throw some band-aids all over myself?

I left without answers, frustrated and uncomfortable, and head back to hang out in the privacy of my off-campus Victorian-era rental that I shared with 6 of my friends. Off campus living was amazing and we had a great house; we all got along and played on sports teams together at school, worked out together, went out together, and ate snacks constantly. At least I had that safe-zone where I could be myself even though I felt like hiding from the rest of the on-campus crowd.

During this time, and over the 2 years that followed, I was taking 21-24 credit hours of finance while I was going to school. Not because I love to make things hard on myself, but because I had to play catch up from my time interning at Disney World for their college program. My credits never ended up transferring, and since I switched majors after returning from Disney, I was behind my graduating class by about 1.5 years.

I received both an athletic and an academic scholarship to attend an accredited university while I played Division 1 softball, and I knew exactly how fast you could lose a scholarship with poor grades. But this workload was heavy. It'd been going on like this since I transferred in, and with the demands of practice and game travelling, my part time job, and the fact that I was now dealing with a mystery illness that was wiping out all my energy, my grades were slipping into a dangerous territory.

I imagine the stress had a lot to do with whatever sickness was taking over at the time, and after shifting around my class schedules, getting a private tutor, and working closely with my professors, my workload started to feel a little more manageable. Soon after, my mystery illness just sort of … vanished. My doctor was left without a medical explanation and decided that, *"Sometimes God just takes care of it, ya know?"*. That was the first time I'd ever heard a doctor mention God in a clinical setting, but hey, I'll take it. *Heal away, God*. I was headed back home for a month-long winter break, happy to recalibrate without any sickness haunting me.

I couldn't wait to get back to school and see my roommates; one month felt like an eternity from each other. About a week into the new semester in the dead of January, my roommates all went out and I stayed back to study for a finance exam. I was woken up by screaming at my bedroom door around 3am, which I assumed was just post-party drunken nonsense. Until I heard my friend say, *"THE HOUSE IS ON FIRE -* ***GET OUT****!"*

You've probably had people ask you what you'd take in a fire if you had the chance to save something. My answer was always a "photo album" because we weren't rockin' digital storage yet: these were original copies. So, that's what I grabbed, along with my trusty Nokia, as I threw my enormous plush robe on and ran across the freezing front porch, dialing 9-1-1.

I only saw two of my six roommates out front among the growing crowd of neighbors, but only one person was away from home that night, which meant there were still three people left inside. I did the thing you *never* do and ran back into the house to grab one of my sleeping friends from bed, screaming for them to get out of the house.

The fire was spreading.

I balled up a towel and shoved it to my face as I crouched up the stairs as far as I could to scream for the others. In what still feels like a miracle, we all got out alive with only minor smoke inhalation and some singed skin and hair. We were all ok. Kind of.

We watched silently from a neighbor's yard as the firefighters worked to contain the angry flames that were crackling and consuming our safe place, full of memories and fun. I realized then that I'd had a growing sense of instability ever since my health and grades started to fall apart. Now my home was, quite literally, falling apart. The heaviness of these compounding challenges was inviting me to look at just how little control I had in my life.

My boyfriend at the time was pretty incredible. I'd never hung out with someone I'd ever been able to laugh as hard with or feel fully myself around. He was a D1 athlete too, so we both understood each others' commitments and schedules. It was a cinematic-style relationship in textbook too-good-to-be-true format; except without the obnoxious public displays of affection and toxic obsession. Think Ryan Reynolds and Blake Lively (personalities and comedic relationship style is where the comparison ends).

Until I found out that he had another perfect match from his hometown, and they'd been together for three years before he and I even met. So it turned out *I* was the "other woman". After I fought back nausea about this new discovery for the next few days, I reached out to the girlfriend. She was surprisingly receptive as we compared notes over the last year to discover dozens of other lies he'd layered into the deception. There was really only one other thing to do…

Go hang out with her.

After a weekend at her college, going out to clubs, staying up late and bonding, we decided we were done with him. Except I was the only one who never saw him again and she would take him back. She wasn't ready to let go. The contrast of our choices made me feel so much stronger than before, but having been on such a high from our fantasy relationship, it took me a while to heal from it's decay and learn how to cope with this new brand of betrayal. I never fully dealt with it since the disruption and chaos of this chaotic season in my life wasn't over just yet.

My brother called to tell me that our other brother had been arrested and that he was in one of the worst jails on the east coast, while he waited for his arraignment process.

"For WHAT?!", I spit out.

Our brother was smart, the life of the party at *every* party he went to, plus he was kind to everyone. So, in what universe was he even arrested, let alone sitting in an actual jail cell? The phone call continued and he told me that, after a night out with friends near his college, instead of driving home, he was going to stay parked while he slept off the drinks. It was winter, so the engine was running for heat. The cops didn't care. He was arrested, cuffed, and given a courtesy ride from the patrol car all the way to booking.

My brother wasn't just the life of the party, he was also extremely sensitive. He was very handsome. Clean cut. Ya know, basically a neon target in a jail with a violent reputation. I was terrified for him. Sick to my stomach, we all were. And I couldn't help, I wasn't even allowed to call him. There was absolutely nothing I could do for him.

Eventually, he was released and somehow, he'd managed to navigate through the humiliation and mistreatment in jail without any lasting traumatic interactions with other inmates. But I couldn't keep tabs on him or see him often since he was living several states away from me. I needed to give him a hug and I didn't know when I'd be able to see him next.

All of this felt like such an extreme departure from what seemed available for our family. It felt like we were dematerializing, like the photo of Marty McFly's family in *Back to the Future*.

Desperate for a deep breath wherever I could find it, I became a bit of a regular at our university's retreat center, Mt. Iranaeus, run by the Franciscan friars from our school. It's tucked away in the mountains not far from campus and I'd go there to study in the quiet and think deep thoughts.

I visited their little chapel with the enormous wall-sized window that looked out into the mountain valley, as I learned what meditation was for the first time in my life. The friars were always so generous and welcoming, feeding us visitors some of the best meals we'd ever had. They were grateful that the mountain was being used to help people who needed to find peace, meaning, or connection. That place *always* delivered.

One of the friars, Father Dan Riley, played a pivotal role in my life while I was there. Although I was attending a Catholic University, I wasn't a Catholic and hadn't grown up with a family who attended church services anywhere. I'd always believed in God since I can remember but I didn't have any sense of what deep faith was supposed to look or feel like.

Father Dan hosted a 3-day retreat for students to learn more about what faith could do in their lives along with all the ways it could benefit the internal struggles we battled with. This felt like exactly the kind of thing I needed to try. At the time of this retreat, my parents were preparing for divorce. The family and home structure I'd always known was now, also, falling apart. It felt like this season of sadness, pain, fear, and disillusionment was getting dished out in unfair doses and way past a reasonable expiration date. I was desperate for anything to restore the hope that was being siphoned out of me and offer a little stability, if only for a weekend.

This retreat provided a healthy pause and the instruction I needed to gain a perspective that would shift the load of my heavy emotions, which had stockpiled during this season of unraveling. To be specific, it wasn't the retreat, it was the clarity through the experience of the retreat that brought me the hope. It was the practical examples of what God had done in my life, and what he *keeps* doing. It was through learning more about what the bible *actually* says, and why the teachings inside it are never something to be afraid of.

I left the mountain that weekend feeling loved, hopeful, and intentional. And I'd need it, because in the next couple months, I'd get a phone call that would leave me grasping for all the hope I could find.

Another phone call. The person on the other end of the line told me that my parents had been in a hit-and-run accident on an open highway in Oklahoma, and they were being treated for severe injuries in the ICU. That was all they said before hanging up. *(Hey Father Dan, got any of that hope and faith handy?)*

They'd been on a two-week motorcycle trip and were expected home the next day.

After chasing down a phone number (yeah, we had caller ID, but we also still had phones that DIDN'T have them, so…) I was able to speak to my mom at the hospital. She told me that they would be ok to come home in a few days or so, and they'd need a ride from the airport.

I pulled up to the arrival zone to pick them up when they landed. They walked through the doors as if they'd aged 50 years: each step taking twice as long as normal. Since the accident had ruined any clothes they'd packed, they were sent home in scrubs. Wrapped in bandages that they were bleeding through, they gingerly got into the car and buckled up. I cried quietly as I pulled away, headed for home to meet the nurse who'd be ready to rebandage the wounds all over their bodies.

After getting hit on a motorcycle on a 75mph highway by a van going 100 mph, being tossed all over the road, skin ravaged and shredded, yet no broken bones or brain damage…

My parents would be ok through what I can only define as a miracle.

I graduated university soon after that. What I couldn't see at the time was that there was so much protection in all of the grit I'd faced in that season. My health was restored, the lives of my roommates and mine were spared, I was kept from a disastrous relationship, my brother avoided any number of potential dangers, my parents miraculously survived, and I'd developed the foundations of a relationship with God that would grow into something so much more powerful for me in the years that followed.

There was so much grace through the gauntlet of that season, but it was so hard for me to see. It was the biggest series of back-to-back body blows I'd experienced in life up until that point; intentionally seeking grace during the pain of all that wasn't something that would have ever come naturally.

But with each small decision to say yes to anything that would give me peace and help me feel purpose, the grace started to reveal itself. Clinging to the belief that there *had* to be relief at some point, I sought out, daily, as much conversation, humor, and connection as I could. Without counter-balancing the crushing discomfort with good feeling experiences, I was sure I'd emotionally collapse under the weight of it all. Those doses of brightness in my day were the little deep breaths that kept me going.

That, and the fact that for each new challenge, if I could do better at focusing on the gift in the pain, it would be that much easier to bear. If I could go even further and trust that the good was already happening *because* of this hard thing I had to experience, I could stay grateful despite my circumstances.

Cuz it turns out, I've never experienced pain without witnessing the grace and goodness in it.

Never.

It's there if we choose to look, and when we do, there will be people watching. They'll get to see you face an impossible challenge, yet they'll witness an inspiring way to get through it.

They'll see the good.

They'll see the hope.

They'll see the grace.

And that's a fire worth spreading.

Author: Sandra Haseley

Intl. Best Selling Author, Keynote Speaker, High Performance Brand and Business Strategist – Sandra is a specialist at helping driven women create better systems and more alignment in their life & business for extra joy, wealth, and freedom so they can keep doing what they love.

CONNECT WITH SANDRA HERE:

www.SandraHaseley.com

SCAN ME!

CHAPTER 2: SURVIVING ME

By: Shiran Cohen

"I wish I was never born." I used to say those words a lot: and the worst thing about it is that I truly believed in every word. For several years I wished I didn't exist.

"What's the point of living in so much suffering?" was a question I repeatedly asked myself, along with pointing out everything that was wrong with me, and all the reasons why planning my own death would be the best solution.

Not anymore, though. Plenty has changed since I started my journey towards becoming the woman who has the courage to write the words on these pages. This will allow you to revisit these moments in time with me, and while it wasn't an easy journey, it saved my life so it's worth every moment.

Just one text message, "*I'm sorry to inform you but we are having my father's funeral today...*".

What?! It doesn't make sense! A healthy man in his early 50's who was successful, funny, and seemingly always in a good mood - so WHY would he take his own life?

Later that day, I was driving home from work and I kept trying to understand why he did it. From the outside it all seemed so perfect: a successful business owner, a family man with loving children, the perfect house, a desirable car, the whole package was right there in his hands.

I took a drive to try and clear my head and search for answers, asking out loud, "Didn't you have any other choice?" to a friend who wasn't there.

I suddenly realized what the question was actually meant for me, so I asked myself, "Shiran, is there another way?"

That was the moment I knew I didn't want to cause any more pain to the people who loved me. I knew I didn't want to carry that blame on my soul. You see, if I would have followed through on the plan I had back then to take my life, I wouldn't be able to tell you this story and, more importantly, the message behind my story wouldn't have reached you.

You probably want to know why I had a plan to end my own life. The simple truth is that I'd just had enough! I felt like I couldn't bear the pain anymore. The emotional and physical pain were unbearable. But the deeper truth is that I was ashamed of who I was. All I saw was the incapable, embarrassing, and unworthy woman I'd become after my car accident in 2013 that left me chronically injured. How I described myself was my own perspective and not a reflection of other people's treatment of me at that time in my life.

Before the accident, I was a successful person in the eyes of others and I was proud of my accomplishments. I served for 2 years in the Israeli military and received a Certificate of Excellence for my role as a commander of 42 soldiers. Following my military service, while I went to school to study architecture, I was hired for defense work, preventing terrorism in aviation worldwide. This job became a part of my identity as I'd developed a personal mission to serve after losing two of my cousins to separate terrorist attacks. My cousin, Maya, was killed in a car bombing in 1994 and my other cousin, Mor, was shot and killed by a terrorist in 2001.

So this was more than just a job for me. It had its perks, too. I was able to travel all over the world and stay in luxurious hotels. Many people I know used to be impressed by that, although for me, it was about making sure I was doing my best to protect each and every passenger on an Israeli flight; it was about making sure they got where they were going safely. The night of my accident, I was driving home from school to pack my luggage for a work-related flight to London which was taking off later that night.

However, I never made it to the airport. I wound up at the hospital, seriously injured, with no idea how long it would take for me to recover. I had broken several bones, suffered a head injury with damage to my occipital nerve, along with an injury to my back spine and neck. I was in a lot of pain, so much pain that I could barely move. Day after day, I took my pills and wore my "tough girl suit", not letting anyone see how much pain I was in.

From a very young age, pain was equal to shame for me, so I did my best to hide it while I looked for answers. I'd been hurt so many times before so healing had become almost too easy for me. However this time, even after the fractures healed, I felt broken.

I went from one doctor to another, while they prescribed medicines for every one of my symptoms. Pills for nerve pain. Pills for general pain. Pills for blood pressure, headaches, and stress. Pills for sleep, for anxiety, and pills for focus because after all those pills I couldn't think straight. Besides the endless amounts of pills, I was clocking hundreds of hours in a variety of physical therapy sessions, mental therapy sessions and pain clinics treatments.

A year after the accident, a neurologist finally delivered my diagnosis. I had CRPS, Complex Regional Pain Syndrome. He told me this condition was irreversible and that I'd be in pain for the rest of my life. Well, so far he's right, the pain has never left.

I was devastated by his diagnosis, especially because a few months earlier I was diagnosed with Post Traumatic Stress Disorder, or PTSD. The combination between the physical pain and the PTSD felt like torture. The physical pain exhausted me each day and so did the need to show everyone that I was okay. Every night when I lay in bed, I was afraid to fall asleep. I was always so exhausted, both mentally and physically, but I also knew what would happen if I fell asleep ... Every night the PTSD would take over and I was reliving the most painful memories from my past: nightmares of massive and traumatic abuse, abuses that I had survived years before my accident. But the PTSD brought it back to life night after night.

While I was driving in the car asking myself, "Is there another way?", I knew that I needed to help myself heal. I also knew that improving my mental health would need to come first. The physical pain wasn't nearly as painful as the pain my mind kept reliving.

I tried my best to find solutions beyond the therapies I was already receiving. I invested years in practicing different methods like meditation, visualization, drinking more water, eating healthier, and understanding the importance of happiness. Motivating myself to do more, to learn and research more so I could believe that I mattered and to find a way to live the life I wanted.

I started to make progress and was able to lower my pain level significantly. Once my pain decreased, I was *finally* able to realize that, in order to heal, I needed to cleanse myself of the shame I kept carrying. I needed to know where this feeling started for me. So I went back to my past...

I was five years old and one of my kindergartener friends lived close by. We were playing happily, having innocent five-year-old fun when, at some point, my friend's younger brother, who was about four 4 years old, started to misbehave. He was running all over the house, screaming, and completely ignoring his parents' repeated requests to settle down.

During his ranting, he'd gotten close enough for me to say something to him as a warning about his behavior. I was so afraid of what the parental retaliation might look like for him, so I pulled him aside and quietly told him, "You better stop behaving this way, otherwise your father will bring out the belt and whip you with it."

The whole room went silent and everyone was staring at me. It was obvious they thought I'd done something wrong, I just didn't know what that was.

His parents asked us all to sit down, they said that their kids should never be afraid of their parents hurting them. Their mother said, "We love our children so we don't hit them. Don't scare them or put those kinds of ideas in their heads!."

I felt so guilty and ashamed, but most of all I felt so stupid for saying it. I didn't realize that other families didn't operate the way mine did. That's when I knew I couldn't let anyone else find out what type of discipline I was experiencing at home.

I remember walking back home, asking myself, "What have I done?"
I was so scared that his parents would tell my parents what I'd said, imagining my own punishment. But thankfully, they never did.

This was one of many life lessons which taught me that it was from that point on I realized that sharing my pain would result in shame from others. So I learned to keep silent whenever someone hurt me. No one ever knew, nor could they imagine, just how bad it really was.

But by sharing my life experiences, I realized that my story is not for me to hide; it's there for me to learn from, to grow from and, more than anything else, to inspire and encourage people to use *their* voice to share their stories and make an impact.

I started sharing vulnerable pieces from my past and giving myself permission to talk about the experiences that traumatized me earlier in life. The things I kept quiet about due to the shame. The very legitimate fear of terrorism which haunted me for years. Growing up in a home full of physical violence the sexual abuse I encountered outside of my household, and all the hurt, blame, and anger I kept in my heart for years as a result.

Being vulnerable was the most unnatural thing for me to do. All my life I was trained to be quiet. I'll never forget the first time I realized there were some things I was not allowed to share.

In addition to my childhood experiences, in every role I worked there was no place for vulnerability; not as a commander in the Israeli military and *definitely* not as a person that had to perform under stress when working in terror prevention. Vulnerability equaled weakness. Of course this isn't true, but at that point in my life, I had nothing but evidence, everywhere I turned, proving to me that volunteering to be vulnerable would destroy me somehow.

I remember the first time I ever sat in front of my psychotherapist and tried to express my emotions to her. I ended up matter-of-factly mentioning events of my past as if they had zero emotional connection to me, like I was telling another person's story, robotic with no emotion. I'd done so much work on myself since then and during my self-healing journey I'd become so committed to, I showed up for my appointment with her and, like almost every conversion we ever have had, she asked me, "What would you like to talk about today?"

My response was always, "I don't know.", with a hint of embarrassment followed by awkward silence. But this day, after she'd ask me the typical, "Would you like to continue our conversation from last week?", I said, "Can we talk about emotions?" She replied, "*Absolutely*, what's on your mind?"

I'd been seeing her for about five years at this point, and she seemed very surprised by my request. She was always careful with her questions because, usually, when she asked me about feelings or emotions, I'd show resistance and often found it either difficult to name the emotion I was having or completely disassociate with the feeling inside me at the time. We began to talk about my past to discover which emotions I experienced back then and how they compared to the emotions I was having at that moment in her office. It felt like we were having a conversation that was half *emotional-vocabulary quiz* and half *test-I-never-studied-for*. Not being able to discuss my emotions properly is hilarious to me *now*, but back then I felt dumb. However, I also knew I was doing my best to get better.

One step after another, we had more conversations about my emotions and I slowly started to find my courage to share outside of the therapy room with friends, until I finally said, “Ok I’m doing it! I’m going to share this part of my story publicly!!!”

I sat in my backyard, placed my cell phone on a tripod, and recorded a video, talking about one of the most painful experiences I’ve ever had. I was physically shaking, I was so scared. A few days later I had the courage to post it in a private Facebook group of just 25 women. Instead of the shame-based responses I feared, the exact opposite had happened. These women were supportive and somehow my story had even touched a few others from the group, inspiring *them* to share their stories as well. I developed strong relationships with some of the women in this group and I'm proud to say they are still my friends today!

Layer by layer, I peeled away the shame from the experiences I went through in life, and instead of pain, I've given my stories the power to serve others through the vulnerability required to tell them. Since doing this, I feel more like I belong and I feel more loved through the strong relationships and connections I've established through helping others open up and recover from their own pain.

Using my life experience and the body language skills that I've acquired through over a decade of defense work, often allows me to see the emotions behind people's words and behavior. It's a great privilege to provide a safe environment for others to share their stories and some people have said it's better than therapy; I feel the same. Impacting their lives and witnessing the massive changes my family, friends, and clients have made by interacting with me adds wonderful grace to my journey.

Sometimes, the little girl inside me is afraid of losing the love and compassion I have today, and at times, it's as though I can hear her say, "Please don't stop loving me, I need you," almost begging for a hug. I won't lie to you, it's a terrifying thought, but I know that no matter what happens next, I will love every piece of this girl until she feels safe. She isn't alone anymore; she has me and I have all the people who are close to me and love me deeply from their heart and soul.

Life is full of crossroads which offer plenty of grit and grace. I encourage you to find the right people to share your journey with, to have the courage to be vulnerable and to heal and inspire others to do the same. There is no reason to suffer alone when you can be loved and accepted just as you are, and to find a better way to live your life, filled with grace.

Looking forward to hearing your story.

Love,
Shiran

Author: Shiran Cohen
Intl. Best Selling Author, Speaker, Body language trainer, Author's Strategy Coach –

Shiran helps guide high performing female entrepreneurs in their life and business by reconnecting more deeply to their own stories so they can make a powerful impact with their message.

CONNECT WITH SHIRAN HERE:
https://msha.ke/shirancohenunspoken/

SCAN ME!

CHAPTER 3: THE ARC OF DECEPTION

By: Tricia Snyder

When I answered the phone at my boutique that day in 2012, I listened carefully to a woman speaking on the other end and instantly fell to my knees!

TRUST me, I'm not the emotional type, *at all*. Too many years of tears early on hardened me. One of my sweet, long-time friends often describes me as a hard candy shell with a gooey center (Yes Joan, *you*!).

ANYWAY, back on track.

It was a phone call I never saw coming. A *mayday* moment, so to speak.
Dumbfounded, I listened while the woman at the other end of the phone said, "Is this Trish?" "*Yes*," I said, hesitantly.
Then the voice replied, "This is Joel's wife."

With my eyes frozen wide, she went on to reveal that the man I was planning to marry in just a matter of months, the man I was living with, the CIA agent who I had kept secret for four years, the attentive and hilarious man I loved, my hero, my very own troop, was actually living a double life.

This woman told me in a subdued, yet direct tone that I was sleeping with her husband, that they had a two-year-old little girl together, and that they'd been married for two years.

I couldn't speak. But he *lived* with me. We'd been together for four years; how could this even be possible?

My closet, *our* closet, was filled with his clothes (some not worth hanging), but seeing his clothes up in the closet always made me feel like he was present, even if he was traveling. I had photos everywhere of us together. My dog was even sleeping on his pillow every night he had to be away, waiting for his return home. The sweet cards he would leave me were always within reach.

As painful and unbelievable as this conversation was, I wanted her to keep talking. I just kept my ear to the phone, breathing rapidly.

I was scrambling to get my thoughts together and somehow, I didn't feel angry. From the tone of voice she was using, I felt she expected me to be defensive, but that wasn't my response at all. We needed to help each other unravel this duplicity of sorts.

I wanted, no I *needed* to know more:
Who was she?
How did she find out about me?
Did he work with her?
Was she young?
Was she an agent?
Did she carry a gun, too?
Was she going to kill me or have someone else do it quietly?
Maybe throw me off a cliff?

Oh, trust me, I had a wild imagination and my brain was flooded with data from the past, trying desperately to analyze what was fact or fiction.

How could I have missed it? Why didn't I recognize the opportunity he had to be with someone with all that time we spent apart? Why was I so naive and trusting?

My mind was trying to come up with answers but I kept getting blocked with the facts I thought I knew that seemed so contrary to the news I'd just heard.

- He hated cheaters. He'd say they repulsed him and he said it so often that I became an absolute believer; so there's no way he could be cheating on me.

- He said he worked for America's Most Wanted one weekend a month (he so disliked creeps), but did he? He was sent to Afghanistan for months at a time and even made me the main beneficiary on his life insurance policy in case anything happened to him.

- During a conversation about combat and all the interest I'd shown in the training they required, he had taken a butcher knife from my kitchen and used me as a "model" while he illustrated how to quickly slit someone's throat. How would he know how to do that if he hadn't been trained?

- He spent weeks in D.C., in and out of buildings where agents were flocking and security clearance was tight. He made me swear to never touch his lanyard or badge.

- In public, he would say he was an I.T. guy, since he wasn't able to admit he was a C.I.A. agent. I always thought that was so humble of him (During this time my brain neglected to remind me that his favorite book was *"Catch Me If You Can")*.

But back to the call…

I still had so many questions and, being his wife, I knew she had the answers I needed.

But my brain was glitching. I felt so incapable of learning anything more at that moment.

Who *was* the "other woman" in this scenario?

So much confusion was clouding my mind. She had the advantage of being prepared for this encounter but I was blindsided.

Months before this phone call, Joel had accepted a job for the C.I.A. which required him to frequent their headquarters in Washington, D.C. So instead of relocating, he decided to rent an apartment there, which made sense, because he was sent there to work for several days at a time each month, coming back home as often as possible. Besides, things had intensified in the war in Afghanistan at this time so trips had been happening much more often. Flying out of the Dulles airport made things easier to get out of the country in a hurry, if they needed him to.

I didn't question a man who traveled for work, why *would* I? Plenty of people travel for work. And it's no secret that C.I.A. agents are real people and those people are bound to have relationships with someone at some point. So I assumed this is what it must be like.

To give a little more context to the state of mind I was in during this relationship, I'd just gotten out of a sad divorce and I'd fallen in love with a younger man. He was wild and wonderful and I found myself feeling joy for the first time in a long time, so I didn't question the blissful escape I'd found myself in.

I also had a tendency to attract and connect with anyone who was non-traditional.

He had guns, big ones, laying around the house. He had maps of backroads in territories only he was allowed to look at, state department booklets and Department of Defense manuals, which seemed to legitimize everything he claimed about his life. His silver Jeep was outfitted perfectly to fit his renegade persona.

I'd always held a deaf ear to anything people said regarding this man's integrity or line of work. How could they possibly know him better than I did? Why would they tear him down like that when they could see how in love I was?

My son, Cody, was also enamored by him. He was 15 at the time and Joel came into the picture with a ton of charm and excitement in a home that needed the kind of spark male testosterone has to offer a teenage boy.

Trust me when I say, it was never boring. I remember when I announced to my son that Joel was moving into our home about 3 months after we met. I let him know we'd be sleeping in the same bedroom. Cody was pretty funny and said, "Cool Mom, I already know what y'all were doing, so have fun." *That* was a relief.

My mind continued to race. I started searching my phone for all the photos of everything he was doing on the days we were apart. They were still there and there were hundreds of them, along with text messages and emails (I *still* have them and choose not delete them for many reasons).

I thought about how we'd talk at brief intervals, and I'd sometimes hear bombing in the background as he told me he was in danger and may not make it out. I rarely slept, terrified I might never see him again.

He even sent a photo taken of him walking down the airstrip in Kandahar holding a wounded warriors flag, which brought me to tears.

He frequently reminded me of his gunshot wounds. He let me know that I couldn't see his scars because the bullet was still embedded in his thigh (which also caused a ricochet off the bone, sending bullet fragments that caused nerve damage… *BLAH, BLAH, BLAH*).

I mean seriously, the deception ran deep.

That man was sharing two beds with two women and had a two-year-old child. He lived in two different states and homes, both owned by women who were independently successful.

We were both footing his bills, buying him clothes so he could look the part, while I took him out to fine restaurants where he'd order the biggest filet, shots of Patron, bottles of expensive red wine, and not let anyone get near us. Not to mention the vacations she and I paid for so he could relax after all the sacrifice he had made for our country.

It was A LOT to grasp in one conversation.

We ended the call and the conversation slowly settled in. After an hour or so I was finally convinced that I wasn't sleeping with some valiant warrior...I was sleeping with the enemy.

Looking back I can see how his Oscar-worthy performance was based on the book *"Catch Me If You Can".* He mentioned it was his favorite on the day we met, which made me buy the book and watch the movie in the first place. But that didn't tip me off. I'd just met him and that was a story a lot of people liked so of course it didn't trigger any alarms.

My brilliant son described it perfectly to me by saying, "He loved being chased knowing that he couldn't get caught. Hiding under masks, personas, and deception like a child playing an innocent game of hide and seek. Except he was the only one playing this game and it wasn't innocent at all; he was leaving victims in his wake. His desires were rooted in the needs of an eight-year-old boy, trying to make someone laugh by playing a game and cry for attention once the laughing stopped. Once people stop chasing him, he'll realize he can't outrun himself and he'll crash."

An analogy that is vivid and true. More from Cody shortly.

In the end, it turned out Joel was never a C.I.A. agent. Not too long after that phone call I'd received, NCIS agents came to my home just like he said they would. They took the computers out and let me know that Joel was an IT guy from the NAVY and that he'd never been out of the country for work (how ironic that the only lie I *knew* he told about what he did was actually the truth, in the end).

He was in a rehab center when his wife found me. He was being treated for PTSD from the chaotic lifestyle he'd created. He was an alcoholic who'd been broken and caught in his own game for the last time.

His wife and little girl came to my home and stayed with me several weeks after we first spoke. We got to know each other, went out to eat, took photos at all the places we went, we cried a lot, but we found time to laugh, too. She is a *gem* - at least he had good taste!

I never heard from him or saw him again. His wife took divorce papers and the photos of us together to the rehab facility and ended their relationship, while he sat there in a state of shock.

I want my son Cody to end this story for me. Here's his take: "He was an actor who took his art form too far. And when you take your art too far, you become a monster in your own movie."

He took it *all* too far, but in doing that, his wife and I formed a bond that will never be duplicated. I've watched her love and protect her little girl as I have my son.

We are FEARLESS WOMEN who stole the next scenes he was prepared to play so other women wouldn't fall prey to his hook.

Turns out we *can* catch you, and we know others will read this story and realize it's time to run as fast as *they* can. It's been years since this happened and now I have my own version of a fairytale ending. I stopped the madness. I found out what I really loved and it was being on my own and running my business.

I knew enough to realize I had control there and wouldn't give up on myself, ever. I was dependable, disciplined, and conscientious when it came to business. I was good at it and I *loved* it.

My business became like the best life-partner I could ask for, and it was right there in front of me the whole time, I just didn't see it. Discovery is a beautiful thing.

I think God had a plan in mind for me to stay focused and steady in order to become the woman I am today (but sometimes I wish He'd been in touch with me sooner about that).

Tradition has us all believing we need to get married, have babies, live in a house with a white picket fence, oh and *definitely* have an SUV! It's the Glass Slipper Syndrome. But not every girl wants the Cinderella ending.

I've worked in fashion for over 30 years, working in LA and NYC, with retail stores in Virginia Beach and Aspen. I'm a jeans-and-boots girl and I've stayed true to that theme, always.

And through it, I've discovered that empowering women to find their true style and confidence is my superpower.

The life I've lived allows me to powerfully mentor women who find themselves stuck in situations or patterns that leave them feeling hollow. I'm able to style these women, while coaching them back into the knowing of their incredible potential. And something happens when "styling them back to confidence"; it's like watching someone come back to life.

I'm grateful for my life, the good and the bad, because I know how the painful experiences have helped shape me and offer wisdom, guidance, love, and support to so many women who are craving it.

I've always kept my personal life private. All people know is that I've worked hard and done it on my own. So in telling this story publicly for the first time, I want to use my voice to remind you to do the things that will support and empower you.

Have a tribe of women who will always be by your side.

Just *do* the thing you keep talking about doing. Don't wait or let fear get in your way.

Live your life knowing that time moves as fast as a cheetah (*my spirit animal*).

Make your dreams a reality by being bold and trusting yourself.

And mostly, be absolutely authentic. Every. Single. Day.

Author: Tricia Snyder
Tricia helps women find their confidence and beauty with a "classy style" that gives them that edge they have always desired.

CONNECT WITH TRICIA HERE:
www.TrishBoutique.com

SCAN ME!

CHAPTER 4: HEAL IN THE HUSTLE

By: Jenni Rae Oates

Rage coursed through my body. Here we were again, neck deep in a heated argument. I knew I would regret this moment, but I couldn't stop the onslaught of emotion rushing out of me like white water rapids.

The dam had broken.
I had broken.

What used to be a rarity had become a familiar scene we'd both memorized. And, as if following a script, I dutifully fell in line, playing my part of the scene perfectly.

Seeing I was not being heard, I bolted out of the bedroom, slamming the door so hard a picture crashed to the floor. I envisioned my husband's shocked face.

"Good," I thought. *"Let him be shocked. Maybe he will finally wake up to our reality."*

I walked into my office, plopped down at my desk, and fired up my laptop. Because that's what strong, capable women do - work through the pain and focus on being productive. The hit I got off of solving, fixing, serving, or helping others was how I powered through hard things. The easy "win" temporarily warded off the agonizing feelings of failure, incompetence, and loneliness I felt in my marriage.

The tears threatened to erupt, but I pushed them back.

I don't have time for this.
I have work to do.
Businesses to run.
People who need me.

Snap out of it, Jenni Rae.

But as my laptop loaded, I was overcome with grief and sadness. This wasn't supposed to be my life.

After 18 years together, I thought we'd beat the odds. 98% of marriages who experience child loss don't make it. We had overcome burying our infant son and navigating 5 miscarriages to build multiple 6-figure businesses together. So how, after investing so much into my family, businesses, and personal growth, was I holding divorce papers and on the verge of a breakdown?

Somehow I thought that getting straight As, being class President, earning a Division I scholarship, and being a pastor's wife would make the ride of life a bit more smooth. But the harder I worked and the more I gave, the more fearful, disconnected, and overwhelmed I felt.

Pushing down the emotion yet again, I turned to my laptop and feverishly began to type. The dreaded wave of guilt I was trying to ward off with productivity hit me like the aftershock from a major earthquake.

This was a category 10 on the Richter Scale.

I couldn't outwork, outhustle, or outsmart this monstrous guilt-wave.

Not this time.

I was out of control.
I felt crazy.
I was completely done.

In that moment, my fingers fell from the keyboard as I was struck with a life-changing epiphany:

I am an addict and "doing" is my drug of choice.

Hustling to be productive and purposeful instantly validated me. Landing a client, achieving the next rank, or creating killer content was the high I needed to carry me through the valley of death I felt trapped in.

I was full-on addicted to "doing" as a way to numb the loneliness and ignore the growing disconnect I felt from myself and others.

Achievements and acts of service had become a cheap substitute for the real version of myself, which had been lost under mountains of urgent demands, expected roles, and suffocating responsibilities.

My flurry of activity and over-responsibility was my desperate attempt to fix *outside* of me what I could not reconcile *inside* of me.

I couldn't bring my son back.
I couldn't fix my marriage.
I couldn't save my kids from pain.

I was good at making things happen, but not that good.

Along the climb to growth and success, juggling a million tasks and attempting to do and be everything, to everyone, had become my way of mitigating the pain of things I couldn't control.

The irony was, it worked.

Mostly.

Most of the time people were happy to let me step up, carry the load, figure things out, or be the glue that held everything together.

And most of the time, it paid me well.

But now, in the silence of my office, I could finally see it was costing me more.

Maybe my super-strength and high-capacity were forms of control that were silently killing me and my relationships. Maybe contributing more than my share to raising the kids, running the businesses, and rallying for my marriage was causing the chaos, not helping it.

A shudder went down my spine as I realized the gravity of my revelation.

The familiar stranglehold of anxiety gripped my chest.

I couldn't breathe.
I was about to break under the pressure.
I wanted to scream from the rooftops that I wasn't OK.
I wanted out of the crazy.

I wanted to break unhealthy control.
I wanted to be free, happy, and at peace.

But what would people think if I couldn't do it all?

Would they think I was an imposter or a liar?

Would being vulnerable and honest ruin us financially?

In that moment, desperation for change trumped my debilitating fear.

I grabbed a pen and wrote out my resignation.

"Effective immediately, I am resigning from the responsibility of anyone else except myself. I will be away from my office for a while, finding a new way to do life."

I walked out, closed the door, and with a twinge of hope in my heart, began devising that way.

For years, I had been learning ways to overcome extreme adversity and rise above. I had spent thousands of hours and dollars in therapy and coaching, collecting pieces of the puzzle for how to live a *Whatever·It·Takes* life.

The pieces I had in place created what looked like a woman who could hustle, go harder, power through, push past pain, make it happen, be it all, and do it all for everyone, no matter the cost.

Using this picture as my guide was killing me and countless other *Whatever·It·Takes* women I knew, so I was determined to find a solution. I grew increasingly frustrated at the years and money I'd invested into pieces that created a picture of a woman who appeared to have it all together on the outside yet was dying on the inside.

The pattern I had experienced is something I call "**The Connection Dilemma,**" which I define as: *An addiction to doing as an attempt to acquire love, value, and connection that always results in the opposite: feeling more unloved, unseen, and disconnected.*

The Connection Dilemma lures high-capacity, driven women in with an empty promise of success, leaving instead a gaping hole of dissonance between the life she longs for and the one she is expected to keep living. Her unconscious drive to *do* in order to receive connection disconnects her further from her true self as she chameleons to be whatever everyone else needs her to be. To combat the shame of living inauthentic and incongruent, she adopts tactics of hiding her perceived flaws or failures, further disconnecting her from herself and others.

I lived this functionally-dysfunctional dilemma for decades. My brand of addiction hid in plain sight, undetected behind the mask of productivity, efficiency, and achievement.

Most women addicted to *doing* are applauded, awarded, and even encouraged to stay addicts by schools, families, churches, businesses, and society. She gets things done, helps others reach goals, and moves companies forward. No one is going to tell the go-getter, problem-solver to slow down or stop.

Too many people depend on her to keep being who she is:

Everything. For everyone. All the time.

But an over-functioning woman typically creates an under-functioning man (or child, or business partner). Why would others step up when she is always stepping in?

While she longs for equal partnership, less stress, and deeper connection with others she feels stuck in a system she partially created and continues to contribute to.

The Connection Dilemma led me to uncover that exact system. I call it "The Crazy Cycle," and the driven, high-capacity woman's default to *doing* will always land her here.

Here is a simple test I created to help you self-identify if this cycle is in play in your life.

You may be stuck in The Crazy Cycle if:

- In spite of all you do, you feel incapable and like you're never enough.
- You are overwhelmed that your world *(home, business, marriage, children)* would fall apart if you weren't the glue holding it together.
- Your daily life looks like a perfectly curated social media profile, giving the illusion that you have it all together, yet you fear people finding out you don't.
- You fight loneliness, dissatisfaction, and frustration despite all your accomplishments.

- You are constantly irritated and triggered and can't stop the over-reactions.
- You and your spouse co-exist and experience little to no intimacy.
- You feel lost among the roles you play and the 5,542 responsibilities you juggle.
- You feel obligated to help others or solve problems, but battle silent resentment for all you do, wishing others would do more.
- You feel exhausted and stuck in "shoulds" and "have-tos" with no clear way out.
- Powering through and hustling is your norm, but you cry yourself to sleep because you long for more.

If you read this list and said "yes" to more than half of them, you're stuck in the crazy.

But don't worry.
You're not alone.

I had my PhD in The Crazy Cycle, so I figured there was no one better than Yours Truly to create a clear plan for how to break it.

After years of grueling trial and error, I mapped out the exact method to stop my own Crazy Cycle, break unhealthy control, and create a life of unimaginable peace and happiness.

Fueled by a passion to see women's lives transformed, I worked tirelessly to create practical tools that could be applied in the moment to effectively stop the unhealthy spiral.

Equipping women with strategies to live each day powerfully and authentically, without sacrificing productivity or relationships, became my mission.

When a strong, capable woman discovers a clear path to do the hard and hustle in a healthy way, she becomes unstoppable.

Nearly 3 years after I wrote out my resignation as the CEO of "Everything to Everyone, Inc." I found myself facing another game-changing moment. Except this time, it wasn't because my life was imploding.

I found myself standing outside, trying to keep perfectly still as the freezing wind whipped around me, so as not to betray the invasion of butterflies that had just overtaken my stomach. The cold combined with my nervousness knocked me a little off my feet. It seemed as if all the moments of personal deconstruction from the shattered pieces of my past had culminated and were being restored into something new, right here in this moment.

I fixated for a solid minute on the shiny ring that was staring back up at me from its cozy, little black box.

I wondered for a moment if people even really understand how much that small circle with a sparkling rock represents. After all I'd been through, I surely did.

So much heartache.
So much overcoming.

So much fear.
So much growth.

So much uncertainty.
So much possibility.

So much.

Was this really happening?
Was he really proposing to me...again?

After nearly 2 decades of marriage, a year and a half long separation, and divorce papers that were signed, notarized, and never submitted, here we were, alone in the cold night air, overlooking downtown Nashville.

The question hung in the air between us.

I know I needed to respond. But my mind was racing.

Would the future be different than the past?
Had we both done enough work to show up for each other differently?
Would our family understand or think this was nonsense?
What would our friends who had walked alongside us think?

This is all so weird! We are technically still married. But we also kind of aren't.

Both of us knew the day we walked in and notarized our divorce settlement that our old marriage had died.

And strangely enough, there was an odd mixture of heartache and hope in that death.

Similarly to the days following the death of our son Hosea, we experienced unbearable pain and grief, while simultaneously feeling hope.

Hope of a resurrection.

For when one thing dies, something new can rise in its place.

Letting go of outcomes - the what, when, and how of the resurrection - is what finally set my heart free to be at total peace, allowing me to live with open-handed trust instead of tight-fisted control. Doing *Whatever·It·Take*s to overcome the hard and hustle of life, but this time, in a *healthy* way.

I snapped back to the present moment and tuned into my heart, something I previously struggled with due to the noise of the crazy, the fear of what others thought, and the frenzied attempts to do it all "right."

Fully connected to my heart and the new version of Jenni Rae, I made my choice.

"Yes!" I said, *"Yes, Yes, YESSS!"*

Although not spoken loudly, my "yes" reverberated across the silence of the cold night air like a clap of thunder.

It broke something.
And set something in motion, all at the same time.

I wasn't just saying yes to getting married *(again)*. This was a defining, "line in the sand" moment.

A "yes" to one thing means a "no" to another.

My yes to this man was also a commitment to myself. I was never going back to how I used to be. I had learned an entirely new way to live the W·I·TLife.

I had finally uncovered the most powerful, authentic, and connected version of myself and I really liked her.

She was no longer living anyone else's life but her own.
She was no longer carrying more than her fair share.
She was no longer exhausted, stressed out, and resentful.

She was happy.
She was healthy.
She was whole.

She was finally free.

Sister, doing whatever·it·takes doesn't have to mean hustle harder, grind more, put your head down, and sacrifice yourself for the sake of everyone else.

My confident "yes" meant I was never again going to allow toxic control, unhealthy over-responsibility, and *doing* to be a drug that dictated my life.

And since that cold November night on a bridge in Nashville, I've been helping hundreds of other women do the same.

I invite you also to step down as the CEO of Everything to Everyone, Inc. and begin to show up for your own life.

It's time to stop the crazy and to step into your power.

It's time to break the trifecta of people-pleasing, performance, and perfectionism and step into freedom.

It's time to toss the script you've been dutifully following and discover your authentic self.

It's time to stop hiding behind the mask of all you do.

It doesn't define you...or confine you.

Let's embrace the W·I·TLife together, and see just how unstoppable you can become.

Author: Jenni Rae Oates
I help driven, high-capacity women heal in the hustle and create sustainable success.

CONNECT WITH JENNI RAE HERE:
www.jennirae.com

SCAN ME!

CHAPTER 5: CHASING THE LIGHT

By: Andrea Costrino

I try to stuff it down and remain unemotional but, as always, my sensitivity chip is stuck on a hair-trigger.

Tears well up as the words, *"We decided to go with another candidate."* are spoken on the other side of the phone.

Bullseye.
A straight shot with perfect precision right through my paper-thin ego.

I was checking emails in my home office when the call came. I listened as the computer screen became blurry and the words slowly slipped behind a curtain of tears. I hang up the phone as my heart plummets straight to my knees causing them to go weak.

Why am I this upset about a job I didn't even want?

Confusion continues as my ugly-cry sets in.

My daughters are on their way home from school and the bus will be dropping them off shortly. I scramble into the bathroom to cover up all evidence of my freshly wounded ego in order to avoid the inevitable question: *"What's wrong mommy?"*

My girls are keenly aware of my emotional tells, especially since I am the crier of EVERY SINGLE Disney movie we watch.

I walk to the bathroom and inspect the damage my face-contorting cry has done. *I'd seen worse.*

As I reach to grab the concealer, feelings of *not enough* begin to fill the bathroom until there's no space left for me to be in it. I evacuate quickly into the bedroom narrowly escaping its suffocation.

Defeat, failure, and regret lurk close behind like a haunting ghost. They forcibly permeate my brain while gathering their reels in preparation for the big show. The projector's light clicks on and flashes of my hasty decisions of the past start playing out in the theater of my mind. This re-run is my subconscious drug of choice, often reserved for punishing myself.

I lie on my bed with fast, shallow breaths and a pounding heart. My heavy eyes start to close as my body sinks into the mattress feeling as though I am slowly slipping beneath the water's surface. I know it's only a matter of time before the inevitable darkness of depression will appear. This is not my first mental illness rodeo.

It's not that I didn't *get* the job.
Not exactly.
It's more about what not getting the job actually represents. It's the realization that my fall back plan was deeply flawed. This job was supposed to be the return to my previous career with more security, a steady paycheck with benefits, a predictable work schedule, dinners with my family, more time with my husband and weekends off; relief for my tired soul. But now that I received this call, it's evident this will not be my reality.

Allow me to set the scene…

After five years of teaching and a boatload of student loan debt, I traded in my smart board for a camera. I knew this could be risky financially and make things harder on our already tight budget at home, but my husband and I were united. The plan was that I'd simply not return to teaching after my maternity leave ended. Instead, I'd stay home with our daughters until they reached school age and avoid the dreaded daycare costs. Then if my photography business didn't evolve, I'd return to teaching and pick up right where I left off.

Isn't it cute when we try to make perfectly-packaged plans for the future?

The real irony of this plan is that photography had never been on my *'what do you want to be when you grow up"* radar. I mean, I didn't even own a camera before the age of 29. But teaching, well... that was something I had dreamed about for as long as I could remember. I struggled to achieve above average grades until I found my passion for teaching in college. Teaching was the ONE and ONLY thing I believed I was actually good at.

As for photography, that started as a hobby. I stumbled upon it while eloping in Italy. My husband and I decided that hiring a photographer was an unnecessary expense for our special day, but purchasing a camera to document the trip: now that sounded like a better investment. It was in Florence, surrounded by tasty gelato, cobble-stone roads and zipping Vespas that I'd discovered my natural eye for capturing the beauty in all things.

Shortly after returning from our honeymoon, we realized that we'd been blessed with our first pregnancy. This is when my obsession with photography officially went into overdrive. Over the next nine months, I compulsively sought information about newborn photography in order to best capture the fresh features of our little one when she arrived.

Once my daughter was born, you never saw me without my camera. I'd follow closely behind my muse, documenting all of her daily activities. By the time she was six months old, my skills as a photographer were taking shape. I couldn't get enough of my new hobby, and apparently neither could my social media feed. Inquiries started to pop in my messenger asking me if I'd photograph their little ones too. I was a bit stunned by this question at first but mostly flattered to find that people actually thought my photos were decent.

Like, people want to hire me to do what I am obsessed with? Jackpot.

My graphic designer husband supported this idea and immediately got working on creating a logo with a name stemming from our wedding in Italy; Vita Bella Photography.

One booked session led to another and over the next year my hobby organically grew into a profitable side hustle. This new business was now running concurrently with my career as a full time teacher, wife, mother of an active toddler, a second pregnancy, as well as the addition of traveling to capture weddings with a childhood friend and photographer living in Boston. This is what things continued to look like leading up to my hiatus as a teacher.

While seeking professional development online, I stumbled upon a photography course with Sue Bryce; an Australian photographer known for her contemporary portraits of women. I adored the way she held me captive with her directive posing cues and motivational words encouraging photographers to charge their worth. I became enamored by her work and desired to try it myself. I set up sessions and practiced with friends who trusted my vision. I fell in love with this genre. I debated offering this type of photography to my clients, but because my website was saturated with children's portraiture, that's what clients continued to book. I had built a reputation as the go-to family photographer in my community and I didn't want to mess that up. I had too much to lose.

As the portrait sessions and weddings increased, my childhood friend unexpectedly moved back to our hometown in Lewiston, New York. We decided to join forces and together, over the next six years, we created a profitable business specializing in family and wedding photography. We spent our days in the studio documenting celebratory milestones, and our evenings chasing the sun while capturing adorable families. On the weekends, we'd travel near and far to click away at happy couples on their wedding day. But it was once the sun set that the bulk of the work came into play. With my kids and husband off to bed, I'd assume the familiar position at my desk and edit images well past midnight. Late night coffees and chocolate-covered espresso beans became my trusted trick in order to place a few checkmarks on my extensive to-do list.

After years of the same routine, burnout began to set in. Our unrelenting schedule, paired with the frustration of a stagnant bank account from undercharging and over-delivering, was starting to chip away at my passion for photography. The guilt of lost moments with my family had become soul crushing; my husband missed his wife and my kids missed their mama. It all started to become clear that this journey had cost too much and earned too little. Months later, I finally hit a stage of burnout that could no longer be resuscitated with any amount of coffee or chocolate.

This is when I reluctantly began the walk of shame back to teaching. I truly loved the dream of owning my own business but the idea of returning to a predictable career was a welcomed plan for my worn out soul. I decided to end my business partnership and began subbing at a local school. The moment a full time position opened up, I got my resume in order and confidently prepared for the interview.

For the job I didn't get.

This unexpected blow, along with the end of my photography business, threw me straight into the depths of a depression like I had never experienced before. My body shut down as my dreams and enthusiasm for life faded to black.

And there I stayed for months...
Ruminating on my perceived flawed decisions.
Riddled with guilt for squandering my degree.
Petrified for our finances and growing debt.
Broken over the loss of a business that I had worked so hard to build.
Devastated that my back-up plan had failed.

In an attempt to see more clearly, I sought professional therapy. With this support, I could feel my body starting to rise slowly toward the sunshine patiently waiting for me above the water's surface. During this time, I devoured every self-help book I could get my desperate, little hands on. When I wasn't reading, I incessantly listened to podcasts geared toward mindfulness and abundance.

I started to feel better, so I added clients back to my calendar to help keep our finances afloat at home. Since I no longer had a studio, I went back to the hustle of chasing the sun and photographing families outdoors in the evening while I continued to miss fleeting moments with my family.

Numbing out on social media one day, the face of a childhood friend appeared in my newsfeed. She was speaking on a LIVE video to women about "finding your purpose". I was instantly drawn in and hooked by her uplifting delivery of valuable information with a side of humor. I immediately reached out.

Mrs. Sandra Haseley spoke life back into me that very day. She listened patiently to everything I was going through and asked some hard hitting questions about my passion and what I really wanted in life. Flashes of Sue Bryce and her portraits of women came flooding back in. I was reminded of my neglected desire to work with women. Over the next few weeks Sandra and I created a plan to build a sustainable career focusing narrowly on women's portraits.

With this fresh outlook, I became buoyant once again. This conversation felt like having a coast guard dive down and pass me the rebreather for a quick hit of oxygen. Along with my husband's support, Sue's mentoring, and Sandra's guidance, I now had a clear vision to do the big work needed.

Over the next month I made many changes...
I restructured my business by establishing much needed boundaries.
I priced my services appropriately by aligning them with professional standards.
I created a family-first schedule to honor my priorities.
I built a portfolio of work in a new studio to reflect my new style.
I rebranded with a new name.
I spoke authentically to my prospecting clients with a vulnerable and heart-driven approach.

As inquiries started to filter in, I could feel the exciting beginnings of forward momentum. My message was resonating with the women in my community. They could see the value in celebrating themselves with a session. I let out a sigh of relief knowing that my pivot was being well-received.

As I approached the launch of my very first photography campaign featuring women over 40 years old, good ol' COVID-19 hit. While the country went into shutdown, I could feel the water at my feet as the tide of despair came rolling back in. Over the next four months, I fought daily to keep a positive mindset, while also trying to figure out how to navigate life during a global pandemic. I took this time to focus on studying posing and lighting techniques, my mental health, and my family.

With five months remaining in 2020 the pandemic released its isolating grip on my business plan. I had two kids at home enrolled in remote learning, a depleted bank account, and a mountain of unknowns, but I launched my new business anyway. I began serving the women in my community the best way I knew how and to my astoundment, I became inundated with bookings.

Amazing women came to my studio desiring a session to document their journey in life. Each one of them pushed outside their comfort zones and tackled their limiting beliefs about being photogenic. With their vulnerability and trust in me, they left feeling more confident than they had upon arrival. The heartfelt feedback from each of them began to soothe any lingering self-doubt. They gushed over the full service experience, and raved about my ability to extract their raw emotions leaving them feeling empowered.

This is when I realized my superpower.

Not just in the ability to take the perfect photo, but more so in how I intuitively held space for women to feel seen and heard during their time with me.

Who knew my hair-triggered sensitivity chip would actually be one of my most powerful traits in the end?

In the third quarter of 2021, my business hit six figures while I served my community of women. With an abundant mindset and a vulnerable approach I know that I am making a difference in helping women rediscover themselves. It's clear to me now that listening to my inner-knowing can be a rewarding decision but not without a proper base to allow for a sustainable career.

I've learned that leading with authenticity creates true and meaningful connections with those around you. I recognize that sharing your life with the ones you love is the most precious commodity that life has to offer.

I have no regrets about the past. I can see now that each one of these struggles throughout my life needed to arrive and

unravel just as they did. That's why it's called a journey and not a destination, after all. So now, I welcome the good, the bad, and the ugly face-contorting cries all the same, knowing that life is not happening to me, rather it's happening for me.
Plain and simple.

I'll never forget all the women I've worked with on this journey. As much as they believe I've helped them, the truth is they saved me. With their love and support, I've found my true purpose, allowing me to live life in color and remain above the water's surface chasing the sun.

Author: Andrea Costrino
I help women feel empowered and confident by giving them the space to be seen and heard while producing legacy portraits they are proud of.

CONNECT WITH ANDREA HERE:
www.andreacostrino.com

SCAN ME!

CHAPTER 6: FROM GRIEF TO GROWTH

By: Joanne Sotelo, M.D.

One busy morning, identical to so many other busy mornings, as I was ready to open a bag of frozen strawberries, I found myself horribly frustrated because I couldn't find the kitchen scissors: "Where the heck could they be? It must have been my mom again." Ever since she moved in with us, it seems like nothing is where it belongs, literally and symbolically. I find myself bothered over the little things, like finding the scissors in her room days later. I realized that my overreacting had little to do with what I could not find, but rather with an internal struggle that I had never experienced before.

Have you ever been humbled by something you thought you had figured out? I have lived a very structured and good life. I did well in school, listened to my parents, excelled at every job; I checked all the boxes. I lived with my parents until I was 25 and finished medical school before moving to Texas. Living so far from Puerto Rico, where I was born and raised, I always worried that something would happen to my parents and I wouldn't be there to help them. I selfishly begged them to move closer to me. They never did.

Then it happened.

My dad was diagnosed with prostate cancer.

He did well for some years, but after a while it persisted with a vengeance. He made my mom promise that she would not tell me or my brother how sick he was, so it wasn't until much later that I'd discovered how little time he had left.

Almost six months after my parents heard the news about my father's terminal diagnosis, my mom finally asked me to call him to check on him. She kept her promise to him; she hadn't given me any details. I spent almost 30 minutes on the phone with my dad, catching him up on his grandkids and life in Texas. He told me about things going on in our old neighborhood in Puerto Rico, and it was really great to speak to him. But he didn't sound the same. He wasn't his usual talkative self. Was he sadder than normal? I couldn't tell.

In all the agony I felt from being so far from my parents, I was met with a small silver lining. My best friend, also a physician, had assigned herself to my father's medical treatment, managing his medical care that would end up going on for weeks. She told me the truth about his illness. His cancer had spread all over.

I was relieved that someone I trusted was taking care of my dad. She'd let me know that he was okay and that he still had some time. "No need to rush over just yet," she'd said. With that news, I planned to go visit him a few months later, with my family.

But less than two weeks after speaking with her about my father, while we were celebrating my son's birthday, I had this sudden paralyzing feeling out of nowhere, almost like a voice telling me, "*Buy the tickets and go visit them...*"

So I did.

I packed my bags, leaving my husband and kids behind for this trip, to see my dad for a surprise visit. It was beautiful. His brother and my brother were visiting too, and we got to celebrate life as a family, enjoying one lovely last meal together.

My father passed away the next day.

While my dad was sick, my mom told me she used to pray, asking God, "Please let him be with me forever. Don't let him suffer. Don't let me be alone when he passes..." She remains grateful that she got two of her three wishes. But I wasn't able to focus on the good as quickly as my mom. The grief I felt from his passing was just the beginning of the biggest shift in my life.

It's natural for parents to end up needing someone to take care of them after hitting a certain age. One of my prayers had always been, "Please let me be able to take care of my parents when they are in need." I knew that my mom wouldn't be able to take very good care of herself on her own after losing her husband at the age of 75. So my husband and I decided it was the right thing to do to invite her to fly back to Texas with us and live with our family.

She accepted.

I got to work packing the home I grew up in, saying goodbye to the place that built me: the smells of comfort, the items that held so many memories, the lamps from the 70s, the hand-painted Spanish tiles, and the avocado tree.

We all started to adjust to a new normal with an extra family member to share our life with. It felt right and everything seemed to start making sense. I was grateful.

A few months later, my mom was diagnosed with dementia. That is when my perfect little world began to shatter.

As a psychiatrist, I deal with patients who have very intense emotions. In order to be the most effective for them, psychiatrists are trained to block their feelings while treating and serving patients. By doing that, I can feel my patients' emotions and be better equipped to help them through that awareness which they often struggle to recognize. This is the benefit I have as an empath who happens to be trained in psychiatry.

This is my superpower.

The drawback of being an extreme empath who is trained to shut down is that my mind blocks my feelings automatically now. Even though I know all the tools to cope with emotions, I had become the patient now, and my grief had messed me all up. I felt as though I had no control over my emotions, which was completely out of character for me. Sometimes we imprison ourselves without realizing that the key was always in our pocket.

I spent my life “doing the right thing”, checking off all the required boxes that are supposed to equate to a responsible and successful person. I grew up believing I needed to be “the good girl.” Beliefs are tricky. They’re thoughts that we’ve heard someone say out loud or thoughts we tell ourselves, and we hear or think them often enough that we start believing them as facts. We convince ourselves that there is no other way.

Before things started to crumble, I thought I had it all figured out. I had the career, the titles, I was the Division Director of Psychiatry, I was married to another physician and had two smart and beautiful sons. I lived in a nice home, I had a great retirement plan..., etc. What else could I need? Why was I feeling so broken?

I was down, anxious, irritable, and worst of all, I was not always aware. I knew that I had to do something about the way I was feeling, but I’d been so used to having it all under control, I think I needed to believe that I was "fine." I resisted all the feelings because they were too painful at the time. What I was not reminding myself of was that we cannot really show up as our best selves and make conscious decisions when we remain stuck in all the negativity. It was one of the lowest points in my life. The worst part was that I believed that I was doing the right thing, by pushing it all down to protect those around me. It was the total opposite. The person I let down the most was myself.

That next summer I attended a personal development conference, and even though I had been a fan of all these topics for decades, it was probably the first time that I really gave myself permission to let my guard down and stay raw and vulnerable. I realized that one of the limiting beliefs I'd held onto was, "I am the good girl". It is not a bad thing, I am proud of all that I have accomplished, but believing in that meant that I *had* to be good. It made me rigid and stuck on a straightforward path that made me believe that I needed to stay in my lane. I wasn't allowed to mess up. I knew that what might have helped me in the past was not serving me anymore.

Growing up my mom would tell me over and over, "just be a good girl." *What does that even mean?* I wish I had asked myself this question earlier in life. However, I did not question her. My mom has been the woman I have admired the most in my life. She is smart, funny, loving, hard-working and always doing more for others than for herself. If she was able to overcome so much in her life and still be the amazing woman she was, who was I to question her? It is the saddest thing to see her mind vanish away, but it is also incredible to appreciate that her loving essence remains.

Taking care of an elderly parent who is ill is not an easy task. Even though I have all the knowledge, and even help patients and families through it, there are countless times I find myself dealing with frustration, rather than succumbing to the sadness. I was afraid that I would crumble down in tears, grieving, not for what was lost, but what could have been. My father is not here physically, and now I am living with what feels like another child. Then, I would feel guilty for having negative thoughts; I kept myself in this cycle of thinking and feeling. I've found myself saying to patients of mine,

"Sometimes it takes a hurricane to bring everything down so you are forced to rebuild with a stronger foundation, instead of taping things up." Well, in my case, a real hurricane had just happened, Hurricane Maria, which literally took over the whole island of Puerto Rico. My mom was visiting my sister during the storm, and I was unable to reach them for 10 days. It was awful.

I had so much guilt that, while I was living my life as usual with electricity and running water, my sister, my mother, and my beautiful island of Puerto Rico were suffering devastating damages. I wish I could tell you that this pivotal moment allowed my frustration to fade away, but it didn't. I am human after all and I'm allowed to experience the entire range of human emotions, and so are you. But this inner conflict helped me realize that I would still choose to take care of my mother all over again.

I let my walls collapse down and asked myself the tough questions.

Who am I?
What do I want?
How do I want my future to be?
How can I show up as my best self?

How can I grow from this experience?
How can I be a good girl, and still get out of my lane?

After answering these questions to myself, I then had to deal with the lie I'd been telling myself for so many years, "*I am a psychiatrist. I am not supposed to still be dealing with grief, or have symptoms of depression and anxiety.*" It turns out that it's true: Doctors make the worst patients. You cannot heal what you are not willing to feel. What was I ashamed of? What was I not willing to think or feel?

It took a whole year before I decided to go deeper with this work and try to heal myself in ways I could not do on my own. I hired a coach and I gave myself permission to be vulnerable, to get back to the core of who I really am and to reconnect with my dreams. To strip away from my title of "psychiatrist" and connect back to "Joanne." I needed to get out of my lane. I needed to work on myself. So I did the work with my coach and I applied myself, doing my best to implement the shifts and improvements I needed in order to find my way back to who I was and to get back the joy and purpose I once had. I wanted to reclaim my true inner self.

Through this self-discovery I decided that I wasn't fully satisfied at work. Sure, I can work with one patient at a time in my office, but it wasn't enough. But the desire to serve more and serve more patients went against traditional medical culture. I was met with peer judgment that sounded like,
``Why would you want to put in all the effort, you are already a doctor?"
"Why isn't that enough?"
"Are you going through a midlife crisis?"

I heard all these questions way too often. I also had the same thoughts, which limited my dream, allowing me to get in my own way. I needed to remind myself not to let the roles imposed by others, learned from childhood or society, dim my light. It all starts with awareness.

What I wish I believed then was that I am allowed to dream big, and so can you.

Knowing that we have beliefs about ourselves and who we are *supposed* to be might have been necessary at some point in our lives, but these old beliefs can keep us repeating self-defeating behaviors if we're not careful. It's critical for each of us to intentionally decide what kind of life we want to live. Warning: Change takes effort.

Our brain is trained to keep us safe, and it *will* get in your way as you begin to shift things. Just know that it does it in a tricky way by giving you distracting thoughts like,
"I don't have time."
"My kids are too young."
"I am too tired."

Your brain knows that change will be required if you're about to go out and seek your dreams. Your brain is built to seek pleasure, avoid pain and take the path of least resistance. Don't feel bad if you believe that you don't have what it takes to pursue your dream. Recognize that you don't have to listen to that voice in your head. Notice if you are telling yourself,
"it is not the right time."
"No one will support me."
"Who would even listen to me?"

Allow yourself to be grateful for the present moment, while aiming high in this process of becoming your most authentic self.

Only you can do what you do, the way that you do it. You are unique and extraordinary. If the seed of that big dream has been planted in your heart already, it is because you certainly have what it takes to nourish it and see it bloom.

Author: Joanne Sotelo
Psychiatrist and High-Performance Life Coach - Helping professional women conquer their overwhelm and create defined steps towards their dreams for a fulfilling and joyful life.

CONNECT WITH JOANNE HERE:
https://linktr.ee/joannesotelo

SCAN ME!

CHAPTER 7: NOW I CAN SEE, I'M THAT

By: Irene Elbie

The phone rang. The caller ID showed a Texas number: my brother, Benjamin, was on the other end, urgently telling me that I had to come back home, that Abel was in the hospital.

Abel was my younger brother, and I hadn't seen him in about four years, and the tone of Benji's voice told me I better not waste any time.

It took 15 hours to make it on a plane from Alaska back to Corpus Christi, Texas, just in time to be there as my brother's soul left the body it called home for 36 years. I am so grateful I was able to be there, but coming home wasn't something I looked forward to. I left a lot of pain behind me when I moved from Texas to Alaska years ago, and I'd done a lot of work to grow and heal from my past. So, although I didn't give it a second thought to come home for Abel, I knew I had to be on guard.

When I arrived, the guard I had put up was put to work. Sad and tense family members were already spreading the news that my only sister wasn't showing up to attend Abel's funeral. This naturally fueled the ever-present animosity within my family. *(I later found out she had struggles I never knew about and being away from the funeral was a choice I'm now able to respect).*

Shortly after greeting everyone, some for the first time in years, the conversation was replaced by the information that Abel had never carried any life insurance for himself. We discovered that even a modest funeral service, with all that's required, would end up costing a small fortune.

My husband and I were able to handle the bulk of the funeral costs, and we were happy to be able to help. It felt like a way we were able to honor him. But my eldest brother, Adam, was also able to contribute to some expenses, while my uncle's wife, whom I'd never even met before this, helped out with what she could too. *(I'll never forget it, Connie)*. These slivers of grace were moments I clung to during this horrible experience.

Six months would pass since the funeral. The holidays were here, and I didn't even consider how much I'd grown. Not until a family member confronted me to say A LOT of things. This woman had spewed a generous amount of untrue and hurtful comments, not only to me, but to my brother, Adam, and my mother. She was my eldest brother's wife. At first, she refused to see me or allow my brother to see me; but I tried to maintain the smallest hope that she might have turned over a new leaf or, at the very least, would reserve any ill will until I was gone. Instead, she stayed true to character and said, "I was gonna help you with the funeral costs but when I found out that some people weren't pitching in, I said forget it."

I truly believe that grace came upon me at that moment, because it would be more in my nature to respond defensively after hearing such an insensitive and inappropriate comment during a time where I was so consumed with pain. But instead, it was as if a muted fog settled over anything else she said. I still have no idea what was spoken after that, if she said anything at all. At some point shortly after, her mouth stopped moving, and in the absence of what should have felt like anger, disappointment, or rage, I felt nothing against her.

I'm grateful for that, since my natural instinct was temporarily removed for me in that moment, but as she turned away, I seemed to snap out of it in time to witness her approach her next conversation.

As she continued to speak, I realized she said these things to my brother too, her husband, and I could see the pain in his eyes. I saw how hurt he felt, listening to his wife allow her ego, hatred, and anger trump his feelings and our pain from the loss of our younger brother.

How could the woman he married have such little compassion or emotional intelligence to behave this way at a time when her husband was so full of grief? During a time when he needed sympathy and love, she had met him with cruelty and arguments in one of his most vulnerable hours of need.

As I processed these interactions over the next several hours, I couldn't help but feel like all the internal work I'd done to heal my emotions and become a better person since moving away was unraveling as years of wasted effort. It started to feel like the hurt version of myself that had escaped the pain of this place was going to come back to life, and emotionally drown in the way I'd almost done so long ago. The thought of sliding back into that person, that helpless, scared, dependent woman, was unthinkable. I am so much stronger now. I didn't want my environment to dictate how I felt, how much I'd grown, or how much worth I knew I had.

But still, my brother's passing changed me. You see, I was bitter, angry, hateful, hurt, unhealed, unforgiving, and cynical. I became full of toxicity. I found myself having both homicidal and suicidal thoughts. I started hanging on with a death grip to horrible beliefs about myself, beliefs that were completely untrue, but couldn't seem to shake.

Only six months after Abel's funeral, I decided I didn't want to go to work anymore. My brother's death shook me and my paralegal job had broken my spirit: that was it. I chose to stay home. I chose my family. I quit my career as a paralegal and cashed out the little retirement savings I had in order to begin my next chapter of life as a stay-at-home mom.

But only after two short months of being at home, the reality of a stay-at-home life became real, REAL quick. The transition from independent career woman to on-duty mom with no breaks was jarring. I started to feel insignificant in comparison to what I used to do each day. I battled with the move I made, whether it was right for me to stay home. I'd spent so many years struggling, working, and trying to find a way to manage my family and career, and here I was living the stay-at-home-mom life, raising my one year old son. Isn't this what I said I wanted?

I decided to commit to the choice I made and fully surrender to everything it included. Because deep down, staying at home really *was* exactly what I wanted. I worked my entire teenage and adult life, my older kids had to be put in daycare because I HAD to go to work to help support my household. This time, I had a choice. I didn't *need* to go to work this round. So, I accepted that I would miss certain parts of being a career woman, but I also chose to remember the parts I hated for every time I started to miss it. And I'd follow up those thoughts by focusing on the reasons I decided to stay at home in the first place. I would look at my son and I felt like I knew that something about this new schedule, this new stay-at-home-work and quality time together, would create the significance I desired in more ways than one.

Not everyone in my life liked that plan or appreciated the way my values had evolved regarding work and home. I made a change and things were different for me now. Certain people in my life backed off, burned off, or faded away.

Now what?

I'm alone. The people I thought were my friends had decided they'd rather avoid a relationship with me than adopt the new path my life was taking - what just happened?

With no one to talk to anymore, I could feel my emotions stirring wildly because of the rejection I had felt: rejection from people who'd said they loved me. I felt like I was spiraling. My new husband was excelling at his job, and rather than praising him with all my heart, I began envying and resenting him. I would watch him proudly return from work and remember how good it felt to be a part of something like that. I remembered how it felt to be around my peers and colleagues, and how good it felt to get credit for being excellent at my job.

So I was back to questioning my choice and even slightly hating who I was. I began believing I wasn't doing enough and that, since I wasn't contributing financially, I was now “lazy”. That I was a “taker”, a “dependent”, not smart enough, and loads of other lies I hadn't believed about myself in a very long time.

I'd done so much work to remove that toxicity from my thoughts. It took years. Yet all those thoughts started flooding my mind and engulfing my spirit, more and more, every day. It got ugly, and it went on like that for almost two years.

In October, 2019, I was still at a place where I couldn't see any way out of the hell I felt I was in. I wanted to get an exit strategy ready. I was contemplating divorcing my new husband, because I just couldn't get over myself, because it wasn't *me*, it was him...Right. So for the very first time in my life, I decided to invest in myself.

I slapped down a WHOPPING TWO THOUSAND DOLLARS for an online course that would help me create something for myself, find my independence, and start over.

I wanted help.
I wanted to heal.
I wanted to forgive.
I wanted to let go.
I wanted to be happy.
I needed to do something to work.

I invested that $2,000 thinking it would give me a way out and, I didn't know it at the time, but through this program, I was about to meet a whole new world of people who would end up helping me heal in a way I'd only prayed would be possible for me one day. The people I'd meet, who'd become incredible friends, would be the reason I was led to this investment in the first place.

These people, who became true friends of mine, who made room in their lives for me without judgment, who believed in me and prayed for me to receive prosperity and blessings in this beautiful thing we call life: these people let me find myself again. I had no idea how much I needed to find *my* people.

I'd never had that kind of love, compassion, or support in my life, so I wasn't really good at receiving it yet either. Learning how to receive love was huge for me. I learned and heard stories from beautiful spirits that have led me here. I learned how to love myself fully. I was never taught how to do that. All I knew about myself were all the things people would say about me and the negative thoughts I'd grown to think about myself.

But I learned that I *wasn't* those things anymore. I wasn't bitter, angry, hateful, hurt, unhealed, unforgiving, cynical, or full of toxicity anymore. I no longer had homicidal thoughts or suicidal thoughts. I wasn't hanging on to the self-deprecating stories I used to believe about myself.

That was NOT me anymore.

The work I'd done, while learning what it means to love myself, developed the grace it took for me to love other people in the same way. When you learn how to respond to cruel or hateful things with a desire for peace, you end up having so much more compassion in the moment. It's easy to forget that everyone has their own demons to battle, and that many of us do it alone. This kind of perspective helps to soften the blow others' words or behaviors were meant to cause you.

You aren't meant to stick around the people who cause you pain and it's not your responsibility to heal them. But you have a choice to offer grace to the people who've hurt you. If you can see the cruel words or behaviors as weapons from a broken soul, you can let them go and love them from afar without regret of the negativity you might have contributed to it if you had reacted out of anger.

Think differently. Speak up. Be brave.

People are going to judge you anyway, might as well let them watch you rise and shine in the meantime. Find your people. Seek out like minded spirits. Surround yourself with only the people who encourage you, lift you, support you, praise your wins and success. People who offer you opportunities, who are happy to see you, who believe in you, who love to have conversations with you, who invite you to go places and do things, who strive to be better than they were yesterday. Because when you know better, you do better.

The things that worked for me, which I invite you to do if you feel led, is to:

Step into your power.
Commit to being fully yourself.
Do the work to figure out who you were created to be.
Follow your passion, wherever it leads.
Surround yourself with people who remind you of how fun, sexy, and vibrant this world is.

And when you do, you take your power back.

I no longer have to work for someone else to make a living. I don't have to leave my home to drive to an office away from my son. I don't have to spend half my wages on daycare for someone else to do the sacred job of raising my son. Instead, I get to do what I'm so great at, on a schedule that works for *me*. I'm blessed to say that I work from home now, as a relationship coach for law enforcement families, supporting the uniquely strained relationships that our heroes on the front-line struggle to navigate as they juggle the intensely different realities of a dangerous world and a family they're trying to protect. I'm now doing exactly what I want to be doing to serve the world with my gifts, and I also get to be the mother and wife I've always wanted to be, at home, raising, teaching and creating beautiful memories with my son.

Author: Irene Elbie
Stay-at-home-mother and Relationship Coach for Law Enforcement Families. they love.

CONNECT WITH IRENE HERE:
https://linktr.ee/IreneElbie

SCAN ME!

CHAPTER 8: DEATH, DIVORCE, AND DUMPSTER FIRES

By: Maria Violante

Since 2001, I have been intrigued by the concept of serendipity. It was sparked by the romantic-comedy hit of the same name, starring Kate Beckinsale and John Cusack. I used to watch it before bed in college almost every night. I loved how a series of unfortunate events would all lead to this perfect moment of pure bliss. There was something so mysterious, romantic, and a bit rebellious to trust that it would all come together when everything appeared to be falling apart.

My childhood was as close to perfect as it gets. I came from a family of two very loving and supportive parents, Martin and Susan Violante. I am the middle of three girls - Mia, Maria, and Marten Rose. My parents showered us all with love and provided us with everything we could have ever wanted or needed. We were thankful for everything we had and understood the importance of hard work. *Grace.*

Growing up, I took ballet and played soccer, basketball, and softball all year round. I remember my parents driving me everywhere - sometimes all of those places in the same day. They always offered encouragement and were friendly with the other parents on the sidelines. *Grace.*

Sundays were my favorite day of the week. Being 100% Italian meant Sundays were for family and food. We would alternate between my grandparents' houses every other weekend, enjoying the company of my many aunts, uncles, and 25+ cousins, where there was never a shortage of food. These weekends created a lifetime of incredible memories together for me and all my cousins. This family tradition ran strong. *Grace.*

My parents worked hard to be able to send all three of us to an elite college preparatory for girls. Nardin Academy is known in Buffalo, NY for its rigorous academic curriculum, competitive sports teams, and a mission of community service. While all of those aspects were amazing, it was the self-development that happened at Nardin that made a lasting impression on me. It was here that I realized the power of being surrounded by strong, supportive, and like-minded women. I became very close with 12 of the friends I made at this school: over 20 years later, the same 12 women still group-text almost every single day. My father always said that sending my sisters and I to Nardin was one of his greatest accomplishments as a father. *Grace.*

After high school, I accepted a partial Division 1 soccer and academic scholarship to attend Canisius College. I was a focused scholar-athlete. I didn't drink or do drugs. I was often the designated driver and always known as "the responsible one." *Grace.*

At the young age of 21, I landed my first teaching job. I taught 7th grade math at a middle school in Niagara Falls, NY. Significant relationships were made that year and mutual imprints were left on the hearts of my students and I. I loved my job. Those *then* 12-year-old children are now 29-year-old adults. I'm lucky that I still have many of them in my life as friends. At the end of that school year, I was invited to take on a new position as a coach for other teachers within the district. I happily took the position knowing it would help me to reach more kids than I could have ever done through a traditional teaching role at the head of a class. *Grace.*

One day in early November, during my first year as an instructional coach, I remember coming home after work and seeing my Dad lying on the couch. He was holding his forehead and attempting to sleep, but couldn't get comfortable. I asked what was wrong. He responded, "They say it's just a sinus infection."

I've suffered from chronic headaches and sinus infections my whole life and I could tell he wasn't suffering from a sinus infection. Until that day, my dad had only ever missed one other day of work in his career as an accomplished and highly regarded New York State attorney, and it was for his father-in-law's funeral. I knew this wasn't good.

Later that week, my sisters, mom, and I took my Dad to the ER; we knew something wasn't right. After some testing, they saw some lesions on his brain. A biopsy done on a later date revealed the worst news possible: my father had the worst and most aggressive form of brain cancer.

The doctor muttered the ugliest series of words I have ever heard, "Marty has Stage 4

Glioblastoma Multiforme." He let us know the survival rate for this particular cancer is pretty much non-existent. He also said it would be six months before our beloved, smart, and handsome father would lose his battle.

On Sunday, May 7, 2006, almost six months to the day, he was gone. He was 52, and I was 23. I no longer liked Sundays. Enter the season of Grit.

As you can imagine, this rocked me right to my core. My father was, and still is, one of the most incredible humans I have ever met. There are people who are glorified when they die who shouldn't be, but my father deserves it all. I have never met a person on this earth who knew him and didn't have something amazing to say about him.

He was an incredible father, loyal and loving husband, thoughtful son, dedicated brother, and ethical attorney. This combination is rare, which means the experience that I had for the first 23 years of my life was also rare. I was given a gift. Although he was taken from us much too soon, I know how blessed I was to have him as a father; so I would choose him and the heartache that goes along with his early death every single day over having a different father who lived to be old and gray. I am lucky to have been one of only three people on this earth to call him, "Daddy." *Grace.*

The next ten years were a blur.

Have you ever had a moment in your life where you thought, "What *happened* here? How is this my life, and how do I get out of it?"

It was as if I was looking at a map, and in the middle was a dumpster fire with a little red bubble stating, "You are here." Awesome.

I was unhappily married.
I started the process for divorce (which would turn into a horrible four-year battle in court).

I was depressed.
I no longer loved teaching.
I no longer loved much of anything.
I felt really unfulfilled.

But I had these two adorable little ginger-haired babes with curly hair, who looked up to me and called me, "Mama." Gemma was 4, Luca was 2 at the time, and they deserved more than the life we were living through.

This was the darkest period of my life. It wasn't just depressing, it was lonely, scary, and embarrassing too. I had struggled so much and I knew I wasn't done. I could tell this season of darkness would be a long one. So much *grit.*

The kids and I moved out of the home that I had just spent the previous two years remodeling every room of. I left with the necessities - two kids and a bin full of clothes. We moved a couple of blocks over into my mom's house, who graciously allowed us to move in with her while I got back on my feet.

About a month later, I woke up not wanting to live another day in this life. The person I'd become was a foreigner. This woman looked just like me, sounded just like me, and dressed just like me, but had none of the joy, laughter, excitement, or hope that the old Maria used to have. A lot needed to change and it needed to happen WITHIN ME.

I turned to something that I'd done throughout my whole childhood, but got away from during my adult life: journaling.

I also knew that I needed to talk to someone. Not just anyone: someone specific. If I could just speak to her, I *know* she could help me figure out how to move forward and start living again. She was near. I was sleeping in her bedroom, after all.

That person was the 10-year-old version of me.

The girl who only ever knew grace, because for her, life was nothing but amazing and magical. I needed to be able to see life through her eyes again.

I would ask her different questions every night.

What is important to you?
How do you enjoy spending your time?
What qualities are you most proud of about yourself?
What are your strengths?
When do you feel confident?
What are your challenges?
When do you feel weak?
Who do you like spending time with?
What do you love about your friends?

What are your favorite memories?
What do you wish you had more of in your life?
What does your life look like at 35?

Each night I furiously jotted down all of the answers from our interview in my journal. My handwriting got sloppier with each word in an effort to keep up with my brain. I didn't want to miss a thing.

Then it hit me.
"That girl is still inside of me!"
And that girl is still inside of *you*, too.

Up until this long and dark season of grit that I'd encountered, I always thought back to my younger self and underestimated her wisdom, but I rely on it now. This process and discovery lit a fire in me, allowing me to use her as a roadmap to move forward and create a life I could love again. *Grace.*

In the midst of my darkest hour, I fell in love - for real this time - to a man who loves me unconditionally and loves Gemma and Luca as if they are his own. This may not have been the family that the 10-year-old version of me was expecting, but it is the family my heart called me to love. Life is better with TyTy, as the kids call him. He continues to push me to do things out of my comfort zone, adding to the collection of my most memorable moments. It certainly wasn't always sunshine and rainbows for us, but we are here now. We made it out alive, and together. I wouldn't want to do life with anyone else by my side. Silver linings are real. Chris Tybor is proof. *Grace.*

Enter 2020. I was still teaching. I wasn't ready to throw it all away just yet, but I was also trying to build my passion project on the side. I knew I wanted to serve women in the online space, but I didn't know how. The thought of being an entrepreneur scared me. I had no idea how to do it, and it seemed too risky for my character. Fear kept me stuck there. The idea was born ten years prior, and I sat on it for close to a decade.

COVID hit. Here we go again; *Grit.*

This season of pressure and discomfort provided me with just enough clarity. My vision of helping women in the online space became a priority. I decided I was going to help women become healthier, stronger, and more confident versions of themselves using improved fitness, nutrition, and mindset habits as the catalyst for change. Boom.

With the help of my life-long friend and business coach, Sandra Haseley, we did just that. I started a free group on Facebook for women to offer support and training in an effort to help them stay sane during this unprecedented time.

I would wake up at 4:30am every Friday and head to our closed down gym. I committed to showing up in a live-stream for the ladies in my community at 6am to workout together so they could accomplish something for themselves before they started giving their time and energy to others. *So much grace.*

As the fall season rolled around, our gym reopened and returned better than ever. I started teaching in a new school, and Gemma and Luca returned to school only two days a week. This meant I was still homeschooling them most of the time. I felt as though I was doing everything, yet accomplishing nothing. The burnout set in.

In December 2020, that little flame inside me that sparked to help women with their health turned into a wildfire that I could no longer contain. It was time to turn my passion project into a career. I started to charge for my workouts, and bundled them into monthly challenges.

I opened enrollment for 40 women. It sold out in a week.

By March it grew to 120 women and sold out in 48 hours.

By the end of that month, I'd left teaching for good. *Grace.*

Are you noticing a pattern yet?

I get through my grit, by meeting it with grace.

For years, I had dreamed of the moment when all of the struggles were behind me. When I was in charge of a life that made me happy. When each of the non-beneficial events would come together into a moment of pure bliss. Serendipity. This was it.

In the movies, you have the chance to see it all come together in a span of two hours. But this isn't Hollywood. It took me 15 years. It was a roller coaster of a ride with some of my life's highest peaks and lowest lows.

During those 15 years, I would remind myself of one truth before going to bed every night, "You're one day closer to this being behind you."

Until one day, I didn't need to say that anymore.

I was no longer in the middle of the dumpster fire. My little red bubble on the map had been relocated to paradise. Only months after I had traded my original career for my new calling, the "You are here" bubble now read, "Key West, FL": a place my dad would have loved. I was there vacationing with my own family. This is real life. Awesome.

As I look back, I realize all of the grace in my childhood was just preparation for what was to come… an adult life of *grit*.

Grit will happen in my life again.

And when it does, I'll be reminded that we don't have to walk through these tough seasons so angry and defeated. We always have the option to *find the grace* and trust that all of these life events are working for us in a way that will lead to our moment of serendipity.

You're one day closer.

Author: Maria Violante
Online Fitness and Nutrition Coach, I help women become healthier, stronger, and more confident versions of themselves using improved fitness, nutrition, and mindset habits as the catalyst for change.

CONNECT WITH MARIA:
https://linktr.ee/Mariavfit

SCAN ME!

CHAPTER 9: FROM BROKENNESS TO BREAKTHROUGH

By: Vanessa Duarte

I fell on my knees sobbing. "Where do I go from here, Lord? I can't do it anymore."

It was a cold Sunday in December when I finally decided it was time.

Seven months prior to this moment, with absolutely no warning, I heard the words, "I don't want to be in this marriage anymore." At that time, I wasn't ready to accept it. How could I have spent the past 13 years building something that was gone seemingly overnight? How would I stand on my own two feet after being a full-time mom (and treating my business as a hobby) for over a decade? What about those babies? They were only 7, 5, and 9 months old. This would change them forever in ways I couldn't bear to imagine. The thought of what divorce would do to my children made me sick to my stomach. I wasn't ready to let go or to accept this storm that had caught me so off guard 7 months prior; so I had spent the following 7 months fighting to revive the only life I knew. That winter Sunday on my bedroom floor, as I sobbed and surrendered to the reality of the death of my relationship with my husband, I prayed, "Lord, I can't do this anymore. I'm done." At that moment, I finally accepted that I HAD to let go if I were to ever move forward and create a new life.

"I. Am. Divorced."

This sounded like words only other people would say. This was never the plan for me. I would marry for life... Who grows up dreaming of a broken family and checking off the "divorced" box on government forms?

As a little girl I dreamt of many things: I dreamt of being a diplomat, of traveling the world, of finding true love and seeing the pyramids of Egypt on my honeymoon. I dreamt of having a family. One dream I surely didn't have was getting my heart broken, seeing my family shattered, and getting divorced. Facing and accepting the destruction of my family dream was a type of pain I had never experienced before.

Accepting my new reality meant that I needed to create a new identity for myself. The truth was, I didn't know how to define who I was outside of being a wife. I was a mom, but I had no idea how to be a mom without being a wife. I was a child of God, I was a fitness trainer, a coach and a health nut, but how could I identify as those things any longer without this central piece of the puzzle - the *wife* piece?

I spent months thinking about my identity and it took me a long time to figure out who I was. I couldn't see it yet. If there was one thing that I was certain about, it was that my pain, the one I was experiencing on the ground through my tears in that moment, would not have a say over my future. Thus, my complete healing was an absolute must. Otherwise, my children would forever carry the burden of having to "make mom happy and make mom ok". Being a broken mom in need of care by my kids was a burden I was unwilling to unload on them. A mother's greatest desire is for her kids to have the freedom to live whole, happy lives. My reason for healing was crystal clear: I had to do it for myself.

More importantly, I had to do it for them.

The parts of the identity that no longer served me had to go. Fear was a BIG one. I had carried it for a long time. The words unlovable and unworthy were easy to pick up considering my own daddy had left me, and my fairy tale family didn't get to have a happy ending. If grit is defined as courage and resolve, through strength of character, I had to find my grit.

It can be quite a challenge to admit that some of the ugliest packages we are handed, those wrapped up in wrinkled, brown paper, can actually contain extraordinary gifts if you are willing to unwrap them. But it can be hard because gifts wrapped in ugly paper make it easy to focus on how ugly the gift looks and it becomes difficult to believe that there's something good inside. Something we could actually be really grateful for. In order for me to look at this ugly gift wrapped in brown paper, I'd need to find a way to forgive and let go of the resentment I held on to. This was a tall order since I was in the thick of my pain. The truth was, the moment my marriage was taken away from me was the moment I started to find myself again. The valley, the darkness, the brokenness gave me no option but to discover who I really was, what I wanted, where I was going. The ugly paper of my failed marriage contained the gift of a journey of faith, self-discovery, and of uncovering lost dreams.

The separation was hard, but by the time it happened, I was resolved, knowing there was no other way. I was ready for it. My biggest challenge with the physical separation was having to hand those precious children to their dad when it was his time with them. Don't get me wrong; I never question the love he has for them, but I had *just* let go of being a wife and I was still trying to work through my new title as "single-mom". So being a mom, then, was one of the only parts of my identity I was sure about. Being a mom will always be the most beautiful and precious part of me. When those three precious children of mine left my arms for the first couple (DOZEN) times, that was when my new reality hit me the hardest. If my identity was ever in need of an extreme makeover, it was during that time. On those very quiet days I had no choice but to search for who I really was.

It was then when I received God's greatest grace. In His amazing love and patience, God reminded me of how HE sees me. I was reminded of who I am; of my great value, in spite of my shortcomings, and of all the people He had already placed around me who were ready and willing to love me and hold me through it all. It was during those days that I realized I was far from alone. I broke down the barriers of fear and doubt and I allowed myself to be loved and supported. And boy, was I *loved* and *supported*.

One day I received a visit from a friend who was living in Japan at the time. She brought me a special gift and proceeded to tell me it's history. Little did she know how perfectly it exemplified my journey. The gift was a necklace from the Nozomi Project. Nozomi, which means hope in Japanese, is a project that originated after a 9.0 magnitude earthquake shook northeastern Japan, causing widespread damage and unleashing a severe tsunami that caused extensive destruction. This project helps women learn how to craft high-quality jewelry out of broken pieces of pottery discovered in the wake of the tsunami. The very broken pieces become a special, one-of-a-kind, valuable piece of jewelry.

As I reconnected to my identity, seeking to model the Nozomi for my own life, I decided to see my journey as an opportunity to take my broken pieces and build a one-of-a-kind piece of jewelry from it all. I delved into reconnecting with my passion and clarifying a new vision for my life going forward. I searched for what I would be passionate about doing that would also allow me to stand on my own two feet; something that would allow me to provide for myself. I never needed to consider this for myself throughout all the years of my marriage, but I now *needed* an income. I couldn't bear the thought of doing something that did not feed my soul. I wanted to impact people. I wanted to serve and help transform lives.

The process of rebuilding my identity meant remembering who I truly was: I was a beautiful, strong, determined, capable, intelligent, driven, and resourceful overcomer. I was a child of God, not given the spirit of fear. If I could live out this new identity, what could be possible in my life? Could long-lost dreams that felt too big for me to seriously entertain finally become attainable?

I was about to find out.

Twenty years prior, when I moved to the US from Brazil, it became my dream to one day work for the United States' top life-and-business strategist and coach. This dream felt too big for this 4' 7" tall Brazilian so I ignored it and went on to do other things; the education, the falling in love, the having babies, the fitness training and coaching, the picket-fence-building.

This new season reignited that 20-year-old dream for me. Though the dream felt too big, I had decided that fear would never again paralyze me. Doing it, despite my fear, meant embracing that growth happens outside of our comfort zone and dreams are achieved in that stratosphere. My lowest low had created a determination to relentlessly pursue that dream and, though I didn't know how I would get there, I promised myself that I would not stop until I'd made that dream come true.

I committed to "*Doing it afraid*". This meant I would continue to act on the commitment of pursuing my dreams, even when it scared me. It meant doing it when others thought I was a naïve dreamer who would need to get a "real job". I got busy. I took massive action. I got certified. I hired an incredible coach (well several incredible coaches because champions have a successful team around them). I learned from the best and surrounded myself with the people who were achieving the results I was after. I worked hard when I was told I should slow down; I had a dream and a purpose so slowing down didn't even feel good. The pace I kept was fueling me and the progress I was making kept my fire stoked. I learned to become quite comfortable with discomfort. That's what elite athletes do and I wanted to play at an elite level in my new life.

I found myself on the floor in the same room where I had sobbed on my knees years before on that cold December Sunday. Here I was again, in tears. But this time, my tears were nothing but joy; I received the news that I'd just got my dream job of 20 years.

I – DID – IT!!!!!

Through God's immense grace, strength, mercy and leading, I had made it to the other side.

Through the support of my mother who stood in the gap as my true rock at every step of my journey, I'd come out of the valley of despair.

Through massive clarity, dedication, and focused action I did it: I followed my dreams and made them my reality! I still pinch myself in disbelief that I get to do what I love every single day; it's a BIG deal. Trusting that I didn't have to settle and that I was capable, as long as I was willing to do what it took without giving up, is a huge deal.

My journey from grit to grace taught me incredible lessons that I'm compelled to share as I know they can bless your own journey just as they did mine.

As I look back, I had fear in my life that was not reflective of a life of trust in God. I had to face my greatest fear in order to learn what grace is, in order to learn what surrender is, in order to learn what faith is. It was through facing my greatest fear that God revealed Himself to me in ways I hadn't been able to understand ever before.

The pain you go through in life can be an unbelievable gift if you're willing to unwrap the ugly outer layer and find the gift and the lessons that are on the inside. Pain is real, but so is our ability to heal from it, learn from it, and use it for good.

Sometimes in life we need to be stripped out of the things we hold dearest, the things that define us the most, in order to truly find ourselves. I had become so wrapped up in being a mom and a wife that

I did not know who I was outside of those roles. The beautiful roles I held so dearly were so important but I had become nothing outside of them. Sisters, when you define yourself by only one or two roles and you are nothing outside of that, you have a problem. No matter how positive your identity is, if it is so narrowly defined that you don't have an identity unless that one thing is taken away, you may find yourself in a tough spot, like I did. Your marriage may not end like mine, and I pray it doesn't, but those precious kids will surely grow up. They'll find who you are and what excites you about life now, so that when they grow up, they're not left with a mother who's lost and broken, without identity or purpose. Discovering your own purpose outside of your children will give them the freedom to grow up and walk independently on their own beautiful journey.

Stop resisting and embrace your season of growth and change. A refining process takes willingness to be molded. A piece of pottery goes through a molding process in order to turn into the beautiful, artistic, unique, valued piece of art it becomes. Diamonds are formed under pressure. Gold is refined by fire. Allow yourself to trust that though the molding, refining process is uncomfortable, you are in capable Hands and you are being molded into something of great worth. The value of a piece of pottery is infinitely more than the value of a block of clay. What gives it the enhanced beauty and value, usefulness and attractiveness, is the process of transformation it goes through. The only way around it is through it.

If you've ever been in a place where others don't support your dreams, please remember: your dream is yours, not anyone else's. Own it as such. They won't always get it and that is ok!

God will allow pain in your life. Not because He doesn't love you but because He does. Who you become is more important than how comfortable you are in the process. Trust the process.

Our path to healing can bless others and pull them through their darkest moments. My relationship with God is the most important thing in my life. My church community is a huge part of who I am. But the truth is, divorce is a topic rarely discussed in religious circles. That means, whether or not you are part of a church, the road through divorce is a lonely, and painful road.

My journey has opened the door for me to extend my hand and support so many women hurting in silence and, because of my experience, I can reach out when I see someone going through it alone. Had I not been through what I have been through, many doors to serve, connect, uplift, support, cry and pray with other women would have been closed.

It all works out for good. I now have the privilege of working with incredible people to help them find their purpose so they can experience the gift of the growth, greatness, and fulfillment they're meant to experience. This is why I encourage you to find the blessings, the grace and the beauty of your journey. There is always beauty if you're committed to finding it. Commit to the relentless pursuit of your passion and purpose.

"Now to Him who is able to do immeasurably more than all we ask or imagine, according to His power that is at work within us." *Ephesians 3:20*

Author: Vanessa Duarte
Results Coach and Business Results Trainer, helping to empower individuals and companies to connect with their highest purpose in order to create impact, massive growth, and fulfillment!

CONNECT WITH VANESSA:
https://linktr.ee/VanessaNDuarte

SCAN ME!

CHAPTER 10: FINDING THE GRACE IN MY GRIEF

By: Trisha Fraley

"He's gone."

It was the first Friday of January in 2019 when I received a call from my mom that will forever be etched into the corners of my mind.

Your brother is dead.

The phrase "being punched in the gut" is used to describe moments like this. Although I've heard the saying before, and even said it a few times myself, I can assure you that there are no words that can describe the excruciating feelings that came over me as the words passed through the phone. I instantly went back through every single lesson I learned over the course of my life in hopes of finding a way to make sense of why my body felt paralyzed in that moment. I am a tad bit of a control freak, so being faced with this unthinkable emotion was not high on my list of favorite things to do.

I prayed.
I yelled.
I called for help.
I did my best to take a deep breath, but couldn't seem to remember how.

The only question I remember going through my mind is: "What happens now?"

Since you don't know me that well, I feel the need to give you a little backstory. I am a southern girl raised in Georgia, the good ol' Peach State. If you were here, I'd invite you onto my porch to have a glass of tea (the sweet kind) and we would talk about the difficult things we've gone through together. So if you would just go to the southernmost part of your mind, pull up a rocking chair and take a deep breath, I'd love to share how the hardest parts of this story are also the most beautiful. I truly believe that life's most challenging moments are packed with the most powerful significance. However, in order to uncover the grace of the situation, you must first be willing to take the journey *through* the fire.

I am no stranger to the "fires" of life. I am the oldest of three siblings and spent the majority of my childhood helping to take care of them while my mom worked three jobs and went back to college. My father struggled with alcohol and was consistently unreliable as a role model. We never knew if he would show up like he promised or if he would leave my sister, my brother and I sitting on the side of the street waiting for him to pick us up for the weekend. Let's just say that money was not growing on a tree in our backyard, and it took a village to help us get through those early years.

When it came time for me to attend college, it was a no-brainer to move away from my hometown. I wanted to start fresh and create a life that looked different from the one I was living. As much as I loved my family, I felt like there was something more for me. Little did I know that "something more" meant new struggles and new life lessons, or as my mama likes to call it...

Building character.

Yes, every time I went through a difficult situation in life, my sweet mama would remind me that I was building character. *What does that even mean?* If you've never looked up the meaning of "building character", I'll save you some time; it means "to experience the ways of the world so that you're equipped to choose which parts of life you believe are worthwhile or worthy to you." Another way I had heard this been phrased is, "in order to build character, the experiences you go through are most likely difficult and painful, but they'll make you a better person in the process and you'll certainly be more interesting as a result."

I'm sorry, what?

Someone is saying that, in order for me to become a more interesting person, I need to go through something difficult or painful. Well, I feel the need to be very real with you for one second. I'm totally fine with becoming more interesting by doing something that's NOT hard or negative. For instance, if I had so much money that I simply couldn't spend it all in one lifetime, I'd have no choice but to give it away to all my friends. I feel like that would make me a much more interesting person.

Can I get an amen on this? Okay, good.

Now that I'm clear on my sentiments, let me remind you that God's story for my life did not involve rainbows and unicorns and endless amounts of money to give away. He chose to refine me through fire. He chose to help me decide what is worthy of living for by helping me survive loss, debt, divorce, drug addiction, deployments, and more hard moments than I'd like to count. Over the course of my life I thought for sure I could survive anything, until I lost my brother.

Enter that gut punch I mentioned before...

I had just moved back to my hometown and my husband and I were getting ready to build our dream farmhouse. It would be our sixth move and the one we actually chose without the military assigning it to us. We had officially bought our own land after years of praying and dreaming. Early on in our marriage our goal had been to let our kids begin kindergarten in the same school system that they would graduate from. We didn't even know if this goal was possible at that particular point in my husband's military career. So when we saw that our dream was actually happening, we projected that 2019 would be one of the most exciting years of our lives. Little did I know what would actually be in store for us.

It was a typical Friday morning in early January when I received a rare text message from my dad saying that he would "call me later". We rarely texted or spoke on the phone, so I assumed his text was sent to the wrong person and brushed it off. It wasn't until I received a phone call from my mother during her lunch break at work at the hospital that I began to worry. Her call during the middle of the day was just as alarming as my dad's text message. I answered the phone and the sound of my mother's voice on the other end of the line pierced through my soul in an instant.

Trisha, it's Tommy. He's dead.

The coroner had called my mother at work to get more information about her son, but my mom didn't even know he had died. The only thing the coroner had to say to her was "I'm so sorry, I thought you knew." My dad knew, but apparently couldn't find a way to tell me earlier that day via his arbitrary text.

As I hung up with my mom, I felt the weight of the world immediately land in my lap. The grief fell over me like a weighted blanket and my stomach began to spin in circles as I cried out for it not to be true. My husband was deployed at the time, so I called him immediately and prayed that he would be able to answer. He did, thank the good Lord, but saying the words, "Tommy died" to him out loud felt like I was wandering into some alternate universe.

If you've ever experienced the sudden loss of a loved one, then you know that there is nothing you can do in the first moments of hearing the tragic news. You can't breathe the same. You can't think the same. The world stops spinning and your mind instantly rushes to find a way to make it not true. You beg that it's not true. Then you spend the next several days, weeks, or even months learning how to live with your new friend, called Grief, who rears his ugly head at times when you least expect it. If you've never had the pleasure of meeting this convoluted character in your lifetime, I pray you never have to. Grief has no system, or process, and makes no sense. Grief is unique to the individual and to the situation at hand. There are no rules for how long he stays around. The only constant you can rely on is the unfamiliar reality you are forced to embrace.

My new reality began with processing how my little brother died of a drug overdose at my father's house. After years of my dad's influence, my brother had entered into the messy world of drugs. My mom, sister, and I spent thousands of hours trying to help him, sending him to rehab, offering him new opportunities, encouraging him, and doing our best to motivate him to walk away from his afflictions, but something kept him intertwined in that very dark world.

Now, I don't know about you, but if "building character" involves experiencing grief through loss, again, I'd rather not. Finding purpose after losing my brother was one of the hardest journeys that I've ever embarked upon. I had to find a way to forgive my dad because I knew that forgiveness was the only way to true healing for me. I spent my weeks trying to find purpose in all the pain and I didn't know if it would ever be possible. Then one day it was like the peace I had begged for finally arrived.

I was at the park with my boys letting them run out their energy and the sun was setting through the trees. Sunrises and sunsets were my brother's favorite and the one thing he would share with his family even when he was in the midst of his greatest struggle. As the sun began to set, it was like he was smiling down on me encouraging me to not give up. I knew at that moment that the purpose in his life and in his death was to share the power of our choices and the consequences that go with them.

Out of all of my "building character" moments throughout my life, my brother's story was the one that inspired me to help make sure his mere 25 years on this earth made a difference. He may have been ashamed to talk about his hurts or frustrations or the parts of life that made him angry, but I will tell his story. I will tell my story.

Telling our stories of how we survived the fires of life is how we help the ones around us to move forward. The purpose of this entire book is to not only help you realize that you are not alone, but to also see that there is grace in the midst of the gritty, fiery, hard seasons of life.

There isn't a lot that you can control in this life, but the one thing you can control is your response. Some people respond to difficult situations by getting angry, some people cry, others numb their feelings by drinking alcohol or partaking in similar substances. My dad chose the path of drugs and alcohol and taught my brother to do the same. When life threw them a curveball, they formed a habit of numbing the pain. Unfortunately their responses cost them their lives.

Shame will cause a person to feel like they should stay isolated and hidden from the rest of the world. Shame is a liar because it convinces you that you should never talk about what's really going on inside. It tells you that people might not accept you if they knew the truth. Shame destroys you from the inside out and keeps you feeling alone. The only way to kill shame, is to *own your story and tell it*.

My story is laced with messy, hard, yucky moments. But it is also wrapped in my desire to choose positivity and grace no matter what. You can choose to see the world through the lens of possibilities and opportunities even in the midst of hard times. My brother's story inspired me to tell you that you are never alone. There is always someone out there who needs you. Your purpose is not defined by what you have gone through, it is defined by how you respond.

Your response to the hardship you have endured can be the answer that someone in your path desperately needs. Strength is built in the fire and, if you look backwards, you'll find that the strength you have today is because of what you have survived up until this point.

Since you are reading this, I bet you have plenty of stories you could share with me here on my porch. Just think about how much you have had to overcome just to be where you are today.

My brother didn't see a different path he could take at the time, so because of him I want to tell you that there is always a way out of your situation. No matter what you're faced with in life or how hot the fire around you feels, I'm here to tell you that, if you let it, fire can build strength.

You are building strength even as you read this book because you see the hope and the grace within each of the unique stories. You also have a powerful story that should be told. The truth is that there is no one like you on this planet and no one responds to life in the exact way that you do. You, my new friend, need to get rid of any shame you are carrying and tell your story.

Don't let your message die because you fear the fire that surrounds you. Look around, friend. Books like this are buckets of water to help you endure the heat of whatever you're facing in life. My brother's death gave me the courage to step out and help women walk through fire. Fire can represent both the hardship that surrounds you and the passion that fuels you. Grace is everywhere if you just open your eyes and look around.

Stop avoiding the pain of what you have endured. In the words of Robert Frost, "The only way out is through." In order to heal, you must first acknowledge what happened to you and then have the courage to grieve, to forgive, and to grow. Just take your next best step forward.

The world is waiting to hear your story of triumph. Please tell it; for the ones who will never be able to.

No matter what you do, *just keep going.*

If you find yourself at a crossroads and aren't sure what's next, there is always a seat at my "porch" for you to work through your next best steps. Thanks to technology, my front porch is accessible online in a variety of forms. I'd love to connect with you on your journey.

Author: Trisha Fraley

I help women to transform the fires they face into the passion that fuels them to live life they've always imagined.

CONNECT WITH TRISHA:
https://linktr.ee/trishafraley

SCAN ME!

CHAPTER 11: RETREATING BEFORE REACTING

By: Milda Sabiene

"How could this be HAPPENING!?"

This was the expression that poured out of me when I opened a letter from the bank. It seemed like I couldn't move and that I'd stopped breathing. I was lost, scared, and couldn't imagine how I would manage this financial nightmare on such a short deadline.

Suddenly, my business loan term of 5 years had been shortened to six months and I needed to come up with over $100,000 for the bank, or my mother would lose her condo.

I had no idea what to do. I wanted to scream and disappear, or wake up and find out this was just a bad dream.

For more than ten years of my career I was working for different companies in top management positions. Financially, they were safe places, because you knew that each month you'd get your paycheck and when you went home you could forget about work and enjoy your life.

But when you're a business owner, everything's different. I'm not just talking about working extra hours or the difficulty of separating business from family life or having a vacation, but the responsibility for everything you do.

In 2006, I left the corporate finance world and started my own business. It was a corporate event and wedding planning business. It went well until the worldwide economic collapse happened in 2008. Corporate clients everywhere cut their budgets and we were forced to close the corporate event branch of our business.

Losing 50% of my clients meant that I was left only with the wedding planning. But working with brides is very interesting. It's wonderful when the bride is cool and relaxed, but when you're dealing with a super tense and controlling bride, the term "bridezilla" starts to make a lot of sense.

I decided to leave this line of business for my colleague to manage. I needed to focus on expanding the business anyway. I decided my company would start offering bridal gowns to sell and rent, but that meant we'd need a retail location for this new operation.

Knowing my clientele and the type of quality they preferred, I knew I needed to secure a franchise agreement from one of the best French brands in the bridal market: that was actually the easy part.

Once the franchise agreement was signed, I needed to find a location for this bridal boutique. After an exhaustive search we found an old house in the center of the city. The location was incredible but the interior was shabby. We decided that as long as we were committed to running and growing this new business for more than five years, the investment into the renovations of our future bridal boutique would pay off. We signed a rental contract with the owners of the property and I started organizing finances.

The investment that we needed to turn this shabby house into a bridal boutique and showroom was about $120,000. To get a bank to agree to lend me this much money to fix up the space, I'd need to mortgage some of my real estate to get enough money for the down payment. Since my family home was not paid off yet, I approached my parents to see if they'd be willing to let me mortgage my mother's apartment to the bank as collateral.

Risking my own property was one thing, but putting my retired mother at financial risk to bet on a new business venture felt as heavy and scary as you'd imagine. Asking my mother in the first place meant I would have a heavier layer of pressure to make sure my business became successful. But I was certain that I'd be able to make good on the loan repayments, based on the repayment terms we agreed to.

Until I got that letter in the mail.

Trouble does not walk alone

It felt like the sky was caving in on me. Everything felt scary and impossible at the same time. My business was at risk.

My mother's condo was at risk.

And I found myself on the brink of divorce.

Why did my world have to collapse all at once?

Even though the thoughts and fears were racing through my mind like high-speed internet, somehow there was stillness in my head. And at the same time, you feel like you're going crazy and you want to curl up in a ball and hide under a blanket. But you *have* to keep moving, even if it's just one step at a time. After the racing thoughts started to decrease in intensity, I was able to reach for some logic. I knew that allowing myself to feel the desperation and panic that was setting in would only hurt my ability to think clearly and come up with a plan. I needed to focus so I could figure out what my one next step was going to be.

People live and people die. The world keeps turning. If you're alive and you want to stay that way, you just need to keep breathing. And this predicament I was in wasn't threatening death. So as long as I was alive I knew I still had a chance.

$100,000 in six months. How was I going to make that happen? I needed to put my emotions aside and start looking at the situation rationally. Time to count.

I divided the $100,00 I owed over six months and looked at the number I got. That was "*just*" $17,000 per month. For me, it meant that I needed to earn 10 times more than I was earning. I couldn't wrap my mind around how that would even be possible. How was I suddenly supposed to know how to earn such a huge amount of money if I'm working for myself as an entrepreneur? If I knew how to do that, I would have done it already.

But what other options did I have?

File for bankruptcy? Actually, that would have been the easiest way to do it (and not as bad as everyone thinks), but it still meant that my mother would lose her home. So this wasn't exactly an option for me.

My brain was working like crazy, trying to think of all the possible options and ways I might be able to get the amount of money I needed to close on the loan. I couldn't let my mom lose her home, but I'd never before been faced with a financial challenge this difficult in my personal life or business, and the thought of magically coming up with $17,000 per month sounded completely unattainable.

Yet, something inside me knew that anything could be possible if I commit as if there's no other way. And to me, there really was no other way. I *would* find a way out of this.

Traps of Fear

Ever since I was a child, I've been aware of the strength of my intuition. My experiences seemed to prove that my intuition would guide me to answers in rough situations. During other difficult times in my life, when I needed an answer or some kind of a solution but I couldn't see it clearly, I would intentionally get quiet and slow down since it's so difficult to find clarity or focus when stress is taking over.

When things get really difficult, the instinct can be to kick, scream, or run away, which is usually born from fear. Fear of losing, fear of being rejected, or fear of not meeting others expectations can bind us. So that can make it hard to imagine, while we're in it, that our one way might not be the *best* way.

Fear can motivate us or paralyze us. Either way, fear definitely narrows our field of vision. Like desperate animals who feel trapped, we want to pound our way out of a cage, failing to notice the wide-open door, because it is difficult for us to change direction under the high levels of stress we're experiencing. And in such moments, no action is the best action.

Previous to starting my events and wedding company, I'd been working full time as a financial consultant. I loved what I did and I was good at explaining complex financial matters to my clients in a simple and straightforward way, which they were always so grateful for. But this was the era of the collapse of the Soviet Union, when so many people were losing their jobs or getting severely reduced compensation in many industries. It was a time where people were rightly suspicious of financial institutions, which is what led me into the bridal industry.

Since I was being intentional about finding quiet time, trying to spark my intuition to provide me with any creative solution for my financial crisis, something came to mind. I thought of a friend I'd worked with years ago as a financial consultant; he was well connected and he'd built great relationships with clients over the years. He'd lost his job around the same time I began planning events and weddings. I reached out to him to see how he was doing and he was in a similar situation to the one I was facing. So, while he was struggling to support his family and I needed to settle this debt, I decided we might be able to come up with some creative solution together.

We talked about some ideas, and, since I was excellent at simplifying and communicating complex financial information and he had such great business contacts, we decided we would be great at consulting for some of the company leaders he still had connections with.

So we gave it a shot and started working together. He organized the meetings while I conducted the consultations and closed the sales. We didn't procrastinate or get distracted with menial administrative tasks. We closed sales and served our clients at the highest level and did nothing but this, the moment we started working together.

After just one month in business together, I almost couldn't believe what we'd done. We had earned $10,000 and $20,000 in receivable income for the following month. The tension I felt about the loan began to ease as I realized that, at this rate, I would be able to repay everything on time.

There is always a way out…

In Lithuania, we have the saying, "There is no situation without a way out". There is always a way out. Always. It's about remembering that you have a choice.

It's a choice to accept a situation with gratitude, to see different perspectives, to understand your limits, and figure out where you can stretch them or come up with excuses about why you are still stuck in the same position.

Even when our neanderthal brain tries to find someone or something to blame, it's still our choice to accept the situation and look for a solution, or sit in excuses. You *are* the only one in control of your brain, after all.

Of course I was scared when I learned about the payback for the loan I'd taken out. I feared that I would be the reason my mother would lose her condo. I was blaming myself for taking too large a risk and I feared I wasn't competent enough to come up with a solution. I was begging God to help me because I felt so desperate. But all these actions were coming from fear.

My pivot point was when I accepted the situation as something that happened for me, instead of *to* me. I became more grateful for all I had, including the difficult situation. Even after solving my financial problem, I still couldn't imagine what treasures it would bring me.

I also learned that the energy of money is very powerful. And it is purposeful. When the goal is reached, the energy (i.e., money) stops flowing. When I repaid the loan, I had no other clear goal of what I needed the money for and, no matter how strange, the sales and cash flow ended. I went back nearly to the same amount of money I usually earned per month.

My financial consultation journey led me to what I'm doing now. Before I thought I was good at business, but I didn't know I could be good at coaching. For me it wasn't about "the sale", it was the privilege of consulting and coaching, and making a difference in their lives. I was coaching people through one of the most intimate elements of their daily lives: themes about money, cash flow, and personal finances. And if I could do it with something as sensitive and scary as personal finance, then I could *definitely* do coaching!

As simple as it sounds, it was the discovery of the year for me!

So, little by little I started my coaching career. I understood that all this time it was in my blood and I always intuitively was coaching people, without even not realizing it.

At first, I started coaching individually. After some time, I started organizing women's circles to help female entrepreneurs and career women to understand and accept their femininity and its power. And how, by learning to do this, they could make an incredible impact on their relationships or and marriage. Soon after, I started organizing retreats for women all over the world. Because I have personally experienced how important it is to *unplug* from the world, business, and even family, to recharge and reconnect with *yourself*.

So now, more than eight years later, I'm fond of helping people dive deep by teaching them to understand their mindset and of how they can create their world more intentionally. I teach them how to connect their business and material life with spirituality and divine knowledge in a healthy and prosperous way by applying a holistic approach so they can thrive in all aspects of life – self-awareness, relationships, and business.

Remember, YOU are able to create your own world! It's your decision and your choice how you feel, how you live, and what you get to experience. Respect yourself and choose wisely!

Author: Milda Sabiene

I help entrepreneurs to dive deep inside and to understand their mindset and how they create their world, so that they can connect business and material life with spirituality and divine knowledge. And thrive in all aspects of life - self-awareness, relationship. and business.

CONNECT WITH MILDA:

www.linktr.ee/milda.sabiene

SCAN ME!

CHAPTER 12: COURAGE TO CHANGE

By: Erin-Kate Whitcomb

I have had a good life. I would even say I am lucky. But I have had massive loss, fear, and pain, all with a family and friend structure that has allowed me to persevere. I have been an athlete, a leader, an actor, a teacher, a student and someone who has been blessed with an unbelievable amount of trust, love and joy. At pivotal times, I have struggled to find my way and have lived my life in pursuit of grace, joy and helping others. Through many life experiences, I have learned courage, strength, vulnerability, resilience and empathy. But it was never easy.

For whatever reason, I have been hard-wired to push through fear. I make myself do things that I don't want to do, perhaps because I don't want to be seen as weak. I have jumped out of trees into rushing rivers, I have taken on assignments that I had NO idea how to complete (and then hit them out of the park), I have performed in front of thousands of people, my best friend died in my house, I watched my sister die in front of me, I have seen my own mortality … and I'm still alive.

I have been told multiple times throughout my life, "you should start your own business". I always thought that was the STUPIDEST thing I'd ever heard; people who do that have a lot of money and/or nothing to lose.

Why on earth would I go out into the wilderness alone??
I don't have what it takes.
I don't have the slightest idea where to start.
I don't know what business I would be in.
It's selfish.
It's too risky.
It's not me.

So I would smile and nod, giggle and squirm, and then move on.

Instead of finishing my theatre arts degree, I dropped out months before graduation to go on tour with a show; I could finish school later. After the tour ended, I had a grand mal seizure on the airplane coming home. I needed to find a job to pay medical bills, so I took a hospital job and, using what I had learned in my [painful] statistics class in college, launched a study within the department of pediatrics to improve patient satisfaction scores. That was the start of the journey that earned me four promotions in six years, ultimately earning the department manager title.

Reaching for even more success, I left the hospital and met with a recruiter who recommended Finance as a great fit for my skill set. Finance?! Ridiculous. Insane. But the pay was great and I found out soon after taking the job that I was really good at it. It wasn't fun. I soon learned that I was hired to be the "bad guy", terminating all employees and closing all west coast locations of my employer's newly-acquired boutique investment bank. When there was no one left to "downsize", I was let go while 7 months pregnant with my second son; I had a severance package and was back on the market. I landed at another national securities firm and continued to perform as an actor and singer.

I learned quickly that bankers stopped taking me seriously when they found out I was an actor. Similarly, actors were confused about my lack of commitment to my "craft" when they learned I had a high-paying job in the financial district. To protect my heart and my ability to grow, I chose to live a double life.

I knew there were companies and industries out there that honored my creativity. A crafty recruiter found the solution: I was hired at a very well-known tech company, with strong ties to Hollywood and the music industry. At this job, I changed how we did just about everything, saving us hundreds of thousands of dollars a year as a department senior manager. I was doing speaking engagements on Corporate Travel Management and Vendor Management. I was going to auditions on my lunch breaks. When I booked a job, I'd take the days off to shoot a commercial, tape a track, or travel to perform at a live event. It all worked - for 3 years.

Then my life changed yet again. I had two opportunities come at the same time - because, you know, life. At work, I had become so relied-upon as a clear thinker and decisive leader, that my boss asked me to take a new position as Head of the Americas. *Why me??* I stared at him like he had three heads. *I think he did have three heads, truth be told. Not everyone could see them, but I could.*

A few days after I had the *Americas* talk with the three-headed guy, my agent called me to tell me about an audition for a national tour with a celebrity, and it would just be the two of us and a piano player on stage. I went to the audition and, lo and behold, among some fierce competition, I got the job. I was thrilled beyond belief! But I was also terrified, because in order to take this role, I would have to turn down the new *Head of the Americas* promotion. This was my version of Sophie's Choice. In the end, I couldn't imagine turning down the tour. I left my corporate job and went on the road. The tour paid about 30% of my current salary, so rather than resigning, I pitched doing my *Americas* role remotely. I was performing at night and free most days, so it could work. But this was when working remotely was risky for employers, particularly to have a senior leader not on-site daily. Nobody was doing it. It was a big fat no.

When I came back from the tour in the fall of 2009, in the height of the US mortgage crisis, there were no jobs for a director-level person like me. I had to hatch a new plan. I needed to get creative. I was hired by a friend to teach acting at a Catholic high school. She knew that I had a job as an adjunct professor at our university - *you know, the one I didn't graduate from? How do I get away with this stuff??* - and that I was an excellent teacher, coach, and director.

I took the job, but this didn't match the salary I'd been earning; so to fill in more hours, I had started a podcast interviewing actors, directors, and producers, took more live performance gigs and took on private audition coaching clients. I also accepted a seat on the board of Northern California's chapter of the Screen Actors' Guild during the SAG-AFTRA merger. I was cobbling together a living. I took on all kinds of gigs and hated the instability of it all. I was scared. I wasn't making nearly what I had made before I gave up my "job" and went on tour.

Frustrated and feeling the financial pressure, another friend told me about a position that had just been created at an independent K-12 performing arts school. I jumped on it. I was now the Head of Performing Arts, yet another job I knew nothing about. What I *did* know was how to take one step at a time. I had been in new circles, new cultures, new processes and new industries before. I stepped out of my fear and into my courage; it's kind of been a theme throughout my life. I stayed vulnerable enough to ask questions, refusing to ever be the "new guy" who acted like they knew everything, and I realized that this was my superpower.

In this role, I produced multiple shows and mentored music, acting, and dance teachers. I had built a real theatre for the school, rolled out a rigorous arts curriculum, and solved some massive "PR" problems that the administrators faced with the parents. After two years, I had solved the problems they had, and ultimately worked myself out of a job.

Here we go again.

One of the parents at that school had seen how I worked, my executive presence and sense of humor, and wanted to meet with me. He wanted to make me his Director of Sales and I responded by laughing and telling him I didn't do sales (*"You've GOT to be kidding me" may have been the response in my head*). He disagreed and said sales were all about relationships and keeping your word, attributes I was known for. It's who I am, it's how I was raised. Since I didn't have anything else lined up and was about to take a trip abroad with my family, I needed to come home to a job. The pay still didn't match what I was making before the tour but it was *a job* and it paid more than the last one. I said yes, once again walking into a foreign industry, and I took on yet another new challenge.

In my first three months as the Director of Sales, I'd closed the biggest sale the 17-year-old company had ever made. I learned to love that job: I had surrounded myself with people who knew the business well, asked questions, listened intently, merged what I learned with my previous experience, and became a master. After 7 years, I had become bored. And, frankly, they were growing tired of all of my new ideas. At that point, the writing was on the wall and I was ready to move on.

Knowing I was looking for my next role, a newer mentor of mine had put my name in the ring to compete for the Head of Sales role at a well-funded agro-tech company. The pay was out-of-this-world and the product was exciting. I went through five interviews over 6 weeks. They liked me and I was the last candidate they had in their pipeline. Even the recruiter was celebrating my certain victory. So I gave my notice at my current job.

The new leadership mix couldn't agree on what they wanted from this sales leadership role, and I was collateral damage. I didn't get the job. Due to my enthusiasm and hard work to win this new role, I had given notice, planned for my successor, "burned the boats" and ... nothing. This had never happened before.

The same friend who had put me forward for the agro-tech job was well aware of my abilities as a sales leader and was now offering me a job within her firm. She had started her own business when she couldn't find the job she wanted and didn't have any options. She had been where I was - capable, experienced, well compensated and too senior to be a new hire elsewhere. Her firm focused on sales and strategy and when I had declined the offer to work with her - although I adore her - she urged me to start my own consulting business. I thought she was nuts. *See a pattern here? All of my mentors have 3 heads.*

As we talked, she told me that if I started my own company, she'd support me by sending me clients that were too small for the services her firm could offer. I thought that was a mighty solid deal. Ever hear that motivational phrase "jump and the net will appear"? Well, she had provided that net. If I couldn't generate the business myself right out of the gate, I would have someone who would hand me some to kickstart me. As it turned out, she never had to send me business.

I started work on my business name and who I would serve. Within 2 weeks of leaving my job/starting my business, I had written four proposals to engage new clients. I started listening to entrepreneur podcasts and talking to other business owners. I learned how to get clarity on what I do and how I do it.

Within the first month, I had signed 3 clients, making $67,000 in 10 weeks. I could see how this could work. I was shocked and thrilled that my "fear" had driven me in a very positive way and that I could actually do this, whatever "this" was going to be! But it continued to shift - how I did things, why I did things, what my purpose was. In the first three months, I had learned that I didn't like consulting; it was a transactional business. You pay me, I offer my advice and a go-forward plan and the rest is up to you.

It was out of balance with who I had always been. I am an immersionist: I learn about your struggles and I inherently begin to care about you, your business and your results. I am not built to just walk away with client money. I have the distinct ability to teach strategy that is directed by courage, resiliency, decisiveness and empathy.

I wanted to earn the respect and trust of entrepreneurs, to make lasting change, to be better, to realize their potential and follow their dreams. I know what fear looks like and I know what it can do to people. This discovery allowed me to get clear on who I'd work with and who I'd never say "yes" to again. I'm now an Executive Coach and business strategist for entrepreneurs who earn a minimum of $5M in annual revenue. With compassion, humor, tough love, the ability to reveal blind spots, and teaching courage to fail AND to succeed, I help those clients manifest their dream businesses.

My entire career life had been spent outperforming expectations, rising to the top, and either losing my job or losing my love for the job: it seemed I was destined for constant change. What I learned is that vulnerability and courage must be learned and practiced. I went through the darkness, the changes, the fear, but I persisted. I have turned a corner and I am learning to embrace uncertainty. I now know how to teach my clients to navigate and move from *pain to purpose*.

Through my journey, school, illnesses, and changes of direction, I know with 100% certainty that everyone has many gifts. Anyone can thrive and be who they were meant to be. I know that I need to work with people who REALLY want to change, are ready and are excited about the journey, and who want to see a new life full of possibility. I am serving people in a purposeful way, making more money than I have ever made because I am helping others to live their dreams, and I now have a work-life balance I had only dreamed of before. Most importantly, I am changing lives. Now, I'm an actor, a business owner, and a life-changer. And I'm not afraid any more.

It turns out that *I'm* now the one with three heads.

Author: Erin-Kate Whitcomb
I help entrepreneurs align their business

strategies with their goals and create sustainable revenue by manifesting success, learning the art of courage, resilience, decisiveness, and creating a positive work culture.

CONNECT WITH ERIN-KATE HERE:
www.working-courage.com

SCAN ME!

...You *CAN* do this...

It was a privilege and honor to work together with this alliance of powerful, loving, and compassionate women. It's our prayer that you've been able to learn, find hope, or feel less lonely in your journey of grit as you've read through these chapters.

While going through the "hard" in life, it can feel like an unfair and overwhelming combo of pain, sadness, and isolation, but we want you to know that the women in this book are here.

If there are any authors you feel like reaching out to, you are invited to do so. Each author has a link to connect with them further, located at the end of their respective chapters. While you can go through tough stuff on your own, your load lightens much more quickly when you let others in to walk the journey with you.

And when it feels like you're strong enough to take any more grit, draw from the strength you've used in the past to get through those difficult challenges. Your own story of grit and grace is powerful and since every season comes to an end, you can count on your difficult periods coming to a close at some point. If and when you choose to share your experience with others, you'll allow your story to encourage women just as the stories within these pages have hopefully encouraged you.

You, my dear, are a MAGNIFICENT combination of *Grit & Grace*.

-Sandra Haseley & Shiran Cohen

STAY IN TOUCH!

To stay in touch with all things Grit&Grace,
scan the code below to join our mailing list.

SCAN ME!

WE'D LOVE TO KNOW...

We wanted to thank you for reading *Grit & Grace*. We hope there was something in these writings that moved your heart, made you feel less alone, or reminded you that there is hope to get through it.

Your opinion is important to us and reviews help us connect the hope and encouragement from these pages with those who might need it most.

You can scan the QR code below to leave a review, and thank you in advance.

You can also send an email with your review to:

gritandgrace.review@gmail.com

SPONSORED BY…

WHITE GROWTH STUDIO
(For Milda Sabiene)

Our mission is to share knowledge, lead women's transformations, inspire and heal money-related energy within.

Our teaching is based on unique programs leading people to complete life satisfaction and abundance. We have developed a unique teaching of 18 Money Energy Laws to awaken natural abundance as well as an 8 archetype course, Woman Worth a Million, dedicated for women. This course transforms a woman's life and relationships from a360-degree angle.

www.whitegrowth.studio

SCAN ME!

AUTHOR BIOS

SANDRA HASELEY - CHAPTER 1

Photo credit: Andrea Costrino & Co.

Sandra Haseley is a Canadian-born American mother of four amazing children who works full time as a business strategist, high-performance coach, international best-selling author, and keynote speaker.

With nearly 20 years in sales and marketing, and hundreds of millions of dollars in sales throughout her career, she now teaches women how to build and scale their businesses. She's guided thousands of fearless and high-vibe women worldwide, into breakthroughs for simpler, more joyful, and wealthier next levels.

As the owner of Sandra Haseley + CO. and founding partner of Generation Impact Consulting, LLC, she's been hired as a corporate consultant for multi-million dollar businesses for program development, training, and workshop creation.

CONNECT WITH SANDRA HERE:
www.SandraHaseley.com

SCAN ME!

SHIRAN COHEN - CHAPTER 2

Photo credit: Andrea Costrino & Co.

Shiran is an Intl. Best Selling Author, Speaker, Body language trainer, Authors strategy coach – Shiran was born and lives in Israel, growing up in a country where terrorism and war are no strangers, she lost two cousins in two different terrorist attacks.

Shiran served two years in the Israeli military and 10+ years of defense work preventing terrorism in aviation worldwide, where she received a Certificate of Excellence in the role. Following a car accident in March 2013, she had to relinquish this role in order to focus on recovering from the injuries caused by this accident.

Shiran helps guide high performing female entrepreneurs in their life and business by reconnecting more deeply to their own stories so they can make a powerful impact with their message.

CONNECT WITH SHIRAN HERE:
https://msha.ke/shirancohenunspoken/

SCAN ME!

TRICIA SNYDER - CHAPTER 3

Photo credit: Allie Aspinwall

Tricia Snyder is the founder and owner of Trish, a contemporary boutique located in VIrginia.

Her background in fashion began in Los Angeles in the mid 70's and then she spent 7 years in NYC working for several designers including Norma Kamali.

She too, knew that being on her own (OMO) would serve her well in life, and that has been Tricia's mainstay.

Today she resides in Virginia Beach with her family and her sweet Bernese puppy, Rocky. Her son Cody is her other Rock and confidant.

CONNECT WITH TRICIA HERE:

www.TrishBoutique.com

SCAN ME!

JENNI RAE OATES - CHAPTER 4

Photo credit: Jody Gray

Jenni Rae is a Nashville, TN based coach, entrepreneur, and mom of 4, raising 3 this side of heaven.

For two decades she has coached thousands of women to launch and scale successful network marketing businesses while juggling the demands of family life.

She now specializes in helping driven, high-capacity women tired from doing it all create sustainable success and healing in their work and relationships.

CONNECT WITH JENNI RAE HERE:
www.jennirae.com

SCAN ME!

ANDREA COSTRINO - CHAPTER 5

Photo credit: Adore Photo Studio

Andrea Costrino lives in her hometown of Lewiston, New York. She is a daughter, a sister, a wife and a mother of two amazing little girls.

She is a formally taught educator turned self-taught professional photographer.

She is the owner of Andrea Costrino & Co. Portrait Photography.

Andrea specializes in helping women break through their limiting beliefs about being photogenic while producing high quality legacy portraits.

CONNECT WITH ANDREA HERE:
www.andreacostrino.com

SCAN ME!

DR. JOANNE SOTELO - CHAPTER 6

Dr. Joanne Sotelo is from Puerto Rico, she is married and has two teenage sons.

In addition to her two decades as a Psychiatrist, she trained as a Life and High-Performance Coach.

Her mission is to bring more mental health awareness and prevention especially for the Hispanic Community.

She assists healthcare professionals with their emotional and mental well-being to regain harmony and avoid burnout.

As a coach, Dr. Joanne Sotelo helps professional women conquer their overwhelm and create defined steps towards their dreams for a fulfilling and joyful life.

CONNECT WITH JOANNE HERE:
https://linktr.ee/joannesotelo

SCAN ME!

IRENE ELBIE - CHAPTER 7

Photo credit: Jeffrey L. Elbie Jr.

Irene grew up in Corpus Christi, TX and has lived in Anchorage, Alaska for the past 21 years.

She left her job in 2017 to focus on family and her passion, which is changing mindsets so that Souls may be free from those untrue and limiting invisible forces before death.

She has found the power within herself to step into her Light to inspire, empower and impact those who crave change, by sharing her life.

Irene is a Knowledge Broker, a Coach and Mentor, she is a wife, an ex-wife, a mother to three amazing sons, a daughter, a sister, and a friend.

CONNECT WITH IRENE HERE:
https://linktr.ee/IreneElbie

SCAN ME!

MARIA VIOLANTE - CHAPTER 8

Photo credit: Andrea Costrino & Co.

Maria lives just outside of Buffalo, NY with her family.

She left her successful 17-year teaching career to coach women from all over the world to lead healthier lifestyles through improved fitness, nutrition, and mindset habits.

She's the mom of two feisty little red-heads who inspire her to keep evolving into the best version of herself, one day at a time.

CONNECT WITH MARIA HERE:
https://linktr.ee/Mariavfit

SCAN ME!

VANESSA DUARTE - CHAPTER 9

Vanessa is a native of Brazil who lives in Maryland (US) with her 3 children and amazing mother.

She is a results coach and business trainer who helps clients around the world design and achieve the next level of success in their personal and professional lives.

Her work includes one-on-one coaching, corporate training and speaking on virtual and in-person stages.

Her empathy, passion and commitment for helping others overcome limitations and reach their goals are the cornerstone of her work.

CONNECT WITH VANESSA HERE:
https://linktr.ee/VanessaNDuarte

SCAN ME!

TRISHA FRALEY - CHAPTER 10

Trisha is a true southern woman who loves good friends, good chocolate, and sunsets. She is a podcast host, motivational speaker, course creator, and aspiring author.

If that isn't enough to keep her busy, she is also a military wife and mom of two boys who is learning the ways of small town farm life in her free time.

Her passion in life is to help people uncover their unique strengths in the midst of life's most difficult situations.

CONNECT WITH TRISHA HERE:
https://linktr.ee/trishafraley

SCAN ME!

MILDA SABIENE - CHAPTER 11

Photo credit: Asta Jasaite

Milda Sabiene lives in Lithuania. She's been through crisis with family and in business, has been married for 25 years, raised two daughters, and has a granddaughter.

She is a business psychologist, holistic coach, and international bestselling author.

She is a life lover and traveler, who organizes goal-setting retreats for women all over the world. She has an energy that is very hard to describe, but very good to feel.

Her power to help entrepreneurs solve problems, to find answers to questions you don't even think you have, and connecting material life with spirituality, is completely phenomenal.

CONNECT WITH MILDA HERE:
www.linktr.ee/milda.sabiene

SCAN ME!

ERIN-KATE WHITCOMB - CHAPTER 12

Photo credit: Cindy Goldfield

Erin-Kate lives with her wife in San Francisco, and their 2 sons are in college.

She has worked as a professional actor, teacher, coach (athletics, acting, speaking, leadership) for over 30 years and is dedicated to helping people grow.

She creates community through humor and is known for her creative approach to life, performance, and meeting goals.

Erin-Kate is a survivor who can find a way to laugh at all of life's pitfalls and turn them into lessons for growth.

CONNECT WITH ERIN-KATE HERE:
www.working-courage.com

SCAN ME!

Thank you for letting us share our stories with you.

From our hearts to yours,

The *Grace & Grit* Author Alliance

Made in the USA
Middletown, DE
10 November 2021